THE IDEA
OF AN IDEAL
LIBERAL
ARTS
COLLEGE

Joe A. Howell
Donald R. Eidson

UNIVERSITY
PRESS OF
AMERICA

LANHAM • NEW YORK • LONDON

Copyright © 1985 by

University Press of America,® Inc.

4720 Boston Way
Lanham, MD 20706

3 Henrietta Street
London WC2E 8LU England

Library of Congress Cataloging in Publication Data

Howell, Joe A.
  The idea of an ideal liberal arts college.

    1. Universities and colleges—United States—
Philosophy.   2. Universities and colleges—United
States—Curricula.   3. Education, Humanistic—United
States.   I. Eidson, Donald R., 1934-   II. Title.
LB2328.2.H68   1985   378'.001   85-22606
ISBN 0-8191-5086-X (alk. paper)
ISBN 0-8191-5087-8 (pbk. : alk. paper)

ACKNOWLEDGEMENT

These beliefs, as expressed in the following pages, are the remarks of a professional lifetime of living and working with students, faculty and other constituencies related to college life. To all of these, expecially the students, we feel indebted. Our thoughts have come from the complex and yet simple interface between college life with students and parents of students as they wrestle with the dilemma of both growing up and learning while in college. It has been through observing and believing in this learning triangle that has given us our direction.

On a personal note, words cannot describe the continued support and encouragement both of us have derived from our spouses, Pan and Mary Ellen. Through their enthusiastic commitment toward making the world a better place through educated students, a motivational force was constantly present. This silent, and sometimes not so silent, encouragement has caused us to have a successful and rewarding experience. To all of those who directly assisted us in the final writing, editing and review of these words, we give our thanks.

Finally, Central Methodist College and its caring community has set the environment from which we have been able to integrate the ideas which seem so right. This special college environment has allowed us to maximize the experiences that fragile under graduates take on their mysterious journey toward maturity through a liberal arts learning experience. It has been hard, but what of importance isn't hard?

Joe A. Howell   Donald R. Eidson

TABLE OF CONTENTS

CHAPTER ONE

A PROGRAM FOR SUCCESS

"Astigmatic perspectives are certain a fact of
life, but I can remember times when things fell
into congruity when someone tried honesty to
arrange them."

Leopold Trymand

How exquisite are the demands of utility at the
beginning of books. The subject of this book is the
liberal arts college. The purpose is to outline a
program for success for the liberal arts college in
the last decades of the Twentieth Century. The approach is to construct a manual and to present a philosophical defense of the manual. The standard for
all considerations is the "ideal" or a consideration
of the ideal. The result is something more than a
list of mottoes (popular these days in industry and
education), but something less than musings on the
state of contemporary education. The particulars
are these:

The ideal and therefore successful liberal arts
college is one

(1) where the greater number of administrators
and faculty share a common vision of what the mission
and goals of the college should be;

(2) where the president has the "people skills"
to focus all contending interests on the campus into
a singleness of purpose, into a shared vision supporting the mission and goals of the college;

(3) where academic integrity and

(4) a clearly-defined system of values form
the foundation for any program or action;

(5) where personalization is the touchstone
in administering, teaching and learning;

(6) where the either . . . or fallacy is avoided
at every turn; and

(7) where the curriculum reflects quantitatively
and qualitatively a commitment to the traditional

1

offerings in the liberal arts.

Jacques Barzun is, of course, right in saying that "no college is ever just right." The model proposed here is "ideal" in the approach, in the constant striving to realize the ideal, not in the ultimate realization, which is deferred to heaven. <u>Such a college will have no identity problems.</u> It will have a soul, a quality that animates all the parts until the whole has a distinctive identity, a character. This "soul" must be as palpable as old medallions to the thumb. It must be felt if not defined; indeed, there will be a willingness on the part of the faculty and administration to work in ambiguity and paradox, to dream <u>and define</u> "without any irritable reaching after fact and reason," as Keats put it. Educators at this model college will not be intimidated by the uncertainties of the <u>purely</u> rational approach to education. Without soul, the college goes nowhere; it is reduced to nothing more than another place offering credits and degrees. Words such as "vision," "values," "quality," and "personalization," given specific application, are the words which define "soul" at the college envisioned here.

The Inverted Prism

The almost infinite number of interests represented at any college, the loyalties associated with the several disciplines, the predilection towards individualism on the part of faculty, the differences in administrative style and substance -- all these must be brought into a singleness of purpose, a clarity of focus, for the academy to be ideal. The energy associated with these interests is often dissipated as people, with their dreams, programs, and objectives flail about in a maelstrom of contending ideas. The interests cancel out each other or lose their effectiveness -- and all for want of direction. The spectrum of interests, with their various colorings, must be filtered through the inverted prism of the shared vision and leave the apex of the prism as the pure white light of common purpose. The person responsible for focusing all of these interests, the prism holder, the one who turns the base of the prism so that all of the colors strike it to emerge as the shared vision, is the college president. At the liberal arts college the role of the president looms large: he is crucial to the success or failure of the "program for success" outlined here.

The Prism Holder

The office of the president at the small, liberal arts college is unique in higher education. No other single position carries with it the immediate possibility of doing so much good or so much bad. The ideal college president must be a "thoughtful" risk taker, one who understands the implications (especially in human terms) of decisions which may effect the very life of the college but is not intimidated by them. He must be an actor, not a re-actor. The profile of this risk-taking president reveals at base an entrepreneur with values, a rhetorically sensitive individual (i.e., a person with "people skills") who has the confidence and compassion to make difficult decisions. His willingness to be a thoughtful risk taker will set the tone for the liberal arts college which must establish--always--an environment of intellectual risk taking.

The personality and policies of the small-college president are pervasive. He is not isolated by an elaborate bureaucracy. His policies and attitudes are perceived--quite correctly--as having an immediate, virtually unfiltered, effect on faculty and staff. The morale of the college can wax and wane with the moods of the president. He can, as perhaps no other individual in higher education can, destroy, rejuvenate, or insure the success of the college. The ideal college, therefore, must have a president whose philosophy, dreams, and preparation match the mission and goals of the college. He must be an academic entrepreneur and creative risk taker; but he must understand, above all, that his principal concern is with "vision," not recruiting, or fund raising, or curriculum, or grants, or any number of things. He must, to be sure, have a highly developed set of "people skills," a commitment to the personal approach, in order to hold up the prism of leadership first one way and then in another in order to catch all of the shades of color which make up his constituency and thus allow the pure white light of shared vision to emerge from the prism. If the president cannot create a community of common purpose, he will have failed. The demands on the individual who can compass this feat are great; lastly, therefore, the ideal college president must have energy, and even more, an élan vital, to be consistently alert in positioning the prism.

Values and Vision

At the center of everything is a system of values which informs and guides all policies and programs. If one might borrow a metaphor from Dante and view the soul of the college as a radiant rose, enthroned at the very center of the rose would be values, and all the row on row of petals surrounding the heart of the rose would be illumined by values. To be ideal a college need not have a "particular" system of values, but there must be a clearly defined realm of values or the college will be without color or conviction. And the greater number of faculty, administrators and curators must subscribe to these values and promote them or these values will become, as it were, academic. To be ideal a college must want to be ideal.

The governing board, the president and the greater number of faculty and staff must want to have an ideal college. Everyone knows by the authority of common experience that if people do not want to do something, they will not, or they will not do it well. One is reminded of the unwilling horse at the water. Oftentimes at colleges and universities, however, faculty and administrators are prevented by their context from knowing what they want. For this reason, the mission and the statement of the mission become extraordinarily important. The mission statement gives direction, but it also serves as the creed that all must emotionally and intellectually accept or reject. It also serves to define for the college community the context of "wanting to" or "not wanting to." If the greater number of faculty, administrators and curators do not believe in the mission of the college, the college will not be ideal. The mission statement is not only a statement of academic purpose but a statement of values, at least at the ideal college. Those who "want" to support the mission statement will translate their partisanship into action, animating the entire college community. This does not mean that there must be a homogenized mixture of people and ideas -- far from it. One would be loath to be identified with an institution of "smelly little orthodoxies," as Orwell put it. But there must be a communality of vision, there must be a greater number in the community who want to share in carrying out the mission and goals of the college, in order for it to have soul.

4

The Touchstone of Personalization

The shared vision is put into action through caring, and "caring" should be equated with "loving" and without apologies. Love is a fragile commodity, and one understands how utterly vulnerable an individual or an institution must be to be so bold as to say that "loving is policy." Risk taking is easier with ideas than with emotions, but without this willingness to risk both the head and the heart, the vision would blur into the common scene found at most colleges and universities. But how is this "caring" put into action?

Personalization of all that happens is the way to show that an individual or an institution cares. Programs, policies, curricula, personnel decisions, student life, everything that touches the college, must be considered by the touchstone of personalization. In order to personalize, the faculty and administration must understand people. And common sense, long abandoned in the academy as too homely for more refined company, should be followed as a guideline.

Like Moliere's character who was amazed to discover that he had been speaking prose all of his life, a number of current commentators on the educational scene are pointing out the desirability of personal contact between teacher and student. The personal approach will be ubiquitous in the college constructed in these pages. Everything will point towards the dictum that "the more often students and faculty are brought together in a personalized context, the more learning will take place." The implementation of this commonly accepted principle is not left to chance, however. Specific policies and programs must be in place to insure that personalization takes place. The more often faculty and faculty or faculty and administrators, and so forth, can meet to converse on a personal basis, the more vital the spirit of the college will be. The "conversational context" contributes to the harmony of the different spheres of interest which make up a college community. There will be and should be tension between students, faculty and administrators as each group works to further its particular concerns. For it to avoid becoming discordant and disruptive, however, the tension must be made harmonious by the process of personalization. Trust and the time to establish trust are the elements which promote harmonic tension. Understanding people is the natural starting point, the place where the fine tuning must occur.

5

The Liberal Arts Curriculum

The faculty of the ideal liberal arts college
will not be so timid as to leave the determination
of the specific nature of the liberal arts curriculum
to anyone but faculty. Certainly students, the least
qualified to determine this curriculum which defines
the very nature of the liberal arts college, will not
formulate requirements. The faculty are the very ones
responsible for mastering, preserving, interpreting
and disseminating that body of knowledge and art and
values which makes up the intellectual and cultural
heritage which, as one commentator observes, "binds
us together as a society." And the liberal arts offerings will be specifically prescribed in content and
quality. Two full years of liberal arts courses, with
the sciences, social sciences, arts, and humanities
well represented, will be required. Beyond that,
specific efforts will be made not to commit the either
. . . or fallacy, that is, the material from the liberal arts part of the curriculum will be integrated with
the material from the vocational part of the curriculum.

The Either . . . Or Fallacy

Administrators and faculty tend towards oversimplification of complex issues in order to formulate
policies that are manageable or defend ideas from a
convincing perspective -- and often unnecessarily ex-
clude vital and helpful ideas and programs. This
problem of oversimplification is compounded by the
tendency of faculty and administrators to polarize
issues as they argue their relative merits. This
either . . . or fallacy is seen in arguments concerning
the curriculum, faculty governance, maintenance of
the physical plant, methods of evaluating the performance of administrators and faculty, fund raising,
church relations (for church-related colleges), recruiting techniques, and so forth. Avoiding the either
. . . or fallacy and subscribing to philosophical relativism are not, assuredly, synonymous. Specific
choices, made on the basis of a system of values incor-
porated in a clear statement of mission, will be made
at the ideal college. But avoiding the either. . .
or fallacy is simply another way of assuring that good
choices will not be overlooked by oversimplification
or blind devotion.

Academic Integrity

The ideal college is one which strives for excellence, for quality. It could not be definitionally otherwise. And striving for excellence involves turmoil and risk taking, but intellectual tidiness is not a virtue since it impedes the striving. Mistakes should not only be allowed, but expected. John Ruskin's doctrine of the imperfect could serve as the model for the program advanced here: individuals who are cared for and who are encouraged in their individuality are inspired to have an intellectual, emotional and creative reach beyond the possibility of grasp. The reaching should never stop. "Excellence," then, may be defined as having a vision and forever striving to fulfill the vision in the ordinary world of everyday experiences.

Alfred North Whitehead observes that "education has to impart . . . an intimate sense for the power of ideas, for the beauty of ideas, and for the structure of ideas, together with a peculiar reference to the life of the being possessing it" (italics ours). Whitehead outlines well what should be in place at the ideal college, especially in the italicized portion of the quotation. Academic integrity and intellectual beauty are addressed in the first part of the quotation, but people and values round out the last part of this peculiarly attractive quotation. The soul is located, after all, in people.

Specific applications of these characteristics of an ideal liberal arts college are made in the remaining chapters as they are applied to considerations of faculty, administrators, curators, and so forth. When given local interpretation and suited to a specific liberal arts college, the following imperatives will lead to a program for success:

CREATE A COMMUNITY WITH SHARED VISION.

SECURE A PRESIDENT WHO IS A THOUGHTFUL RISK TAKER, AN ACADEMIC ENTREPRENEUR, A MASTER OF "PEOPLE SKILLS," BUT ABOVE ALL, ONE WHO HAS THE VERVE AND ENERGY TO BE A SUCCESSFUL PRISM HOLDER.

INSURE ACADEMIC INTEGRITY.

UNDERGIRD ALL WITH A CLEAR SYSTEM OF VALUES.

PERSONALIZE IN ALL CONTEXTS.

AVOID THE EITHER . . . OR FALLACY.

REMAIN DEFINITIONALLY TRUE TO THE LIBERAL ARTS.

CHAPTER TWO

THE IDEA OF AN IDEAL LIBERAL ARTS COLLEGE

"There is an art to make dreams, as well as their interpretations."

Sir Thomas Browne

The presumption evident in the title of this chapter (and this book) is intentional. The very idea of asserting that there is an ideal construct which can serve as the archetype for all of the stone and mortar, dreams and disappointments, curators and curricula, departments and politics, and people and ideas that make up a college gives pause. The problem is not just one of definition, although defining relative and elusive terms brings gray hairs. The problem is that many are intimidated by the ideal, or perhaps more properly, are intimidated by the prospect of having to think about the ideal. The demands of relativism preclude intellectual audacity, but the advancement of an idea or a courtship seldom comes from a timid suitor. One can genuinely subscribe to the idea of intellectual and spiritual humility without being incapacitated. One can acknowledge the imperfections of people and institutions without despairing. The words "ideal" and "idealistic" depend on individual perception for their definition, upon the testimony of the one who has the vision. The ideal college for one, to be sure, may be anathema to another. What is the solution to such a dilemma?

Shared Vision

The answer is that the ideal liberal arts college will be one where the majority of the individuals share the same vision. Although there may be those within the walls who do not share the vision -- and these serve the helpful function of promoting clearer definitions by presenting different points of view -- the greater number of alumni, curators, students, faculty, and administrators must agree upon the mission and goals of the college in order for a college to be ideal; i.e., in order for it to realize its vision most fully. Those who interpret this vision must come from every part of the college community, but the primary responsibility for bringing the vision into focus and for translating the vision into action rests with the college president.

9

Hierarchy of Values

The deterrent to achieving this communality of purpose is, as stated above, intellectual timidity that derives, to quote George F. Will (in a syndicated column entitled "Educational System Poses Danger of Social Disintegration") from "a mistaken doctrine of modern philosophy. It is the doctrine that all values are equally arbitrary, so the 'selection' of values, like the selection of items in a cafeteria, is purely a matter of 'taste.'" The ideal college will not hesitate to admit that it knows what it is doing. It will unabashedly advance a hierarchy of shared values, and these values and the hierarchical principles undergirding them will be reflected in the whole life of the campus, but particularly and most importantly in the curriculum. One will hear talk of "quality" in terms of something that can be understood and quantified. Such studies as George D. Kuh's "Indices of Quality in the Undergraduate Experience," a 1981 study bold enough to advance the idea that there is such a thing as "quality" and that there are ways to measure it and achieve it, will be in evidence in the conversations of faculty and administrators. Evidence of the shared vision and of the gumption to actualize that vision with confidence and certainty on the part of faculty and administrators is seminal to an ideal liberal arts college. The seeds planted and nurtured by those who bear the primary responsibility for determining the idea of the liberal arts college will bear fruit among the other constituents of the college community. But there is more.

The Added Ingredient

At the ideal college there will always be evidence in all the parts as well as in the whole of what Plato might have called the principle of plenitude, a going beyond the expected and the sufficient, the determination to have in any context of the college an added ingredient. When a curriculum, a program, a method, a procedure results as the shared vision is actualized, the next step is to go beyond, to determine the added ingredient or ingredients that will make the curriculum, program, etc., superlative, beyond the ordinary certainly, but even beyond the expected. The added ingredient insofar as the shared vision (the communality of purpose) is concerned is "partisanship." The added ingredient insofar as the ideal is concerned

10

is "the constant striving to achieve excellence."

"Partisanship" implies support with conviction. This ingredient added to the shared vision engenders a zeal for the common cause that transcends the mere subscribing to the mission and the goals of the college. Partisanship promotes the development of community as the partisans share their vision of what the ideal college should be. The college comes alive because the supporters, the partisans, identify so completely with it that they care and because the energy of their convictions will be spent in demonstrating that they care. One hears at every turn protestations from colleges, nursing homes, and automobile dealers that they "care." One doubts the conviction of these protestations and the motives behind them. But "caring" will be evident in the ideal liberal arts college as a demonstrable outcome of the partisanship of those sharing a common vision. Mary McCarthy in her autobiography, Memoirs of a Catholic Girlhood, explains the merits of "partisanship" in a Catholic education, an explanation which may be generally applied to the above. She points out that while children in secular public schools were taught American history, she was taught English history (up to the time of the fat apostate, Henry VIII) because of the bias of Catholic education. She observes: "Granted that Catholic history is biased, it is not dry or dead; its virtue for the student, indeed, is that it has been made to come alive by the violent partisanship which inflames it." The partisan student, she says, feels that history is alive, that it has become "a part of oneself." The partisan students "care" for the lessons of the past because they identify passionately with a cause. Those who share the vision of what an ideal college should be and identify passionately with the college and its mission are partisans. They care.

"The constant striving to achieve excellence" is the added ingredient which stands above all the rest in the ideal liberal arts college, the ingredient that allows the word "ideal" to be fully defined. Robert Persig in Zen and the Art of Motorcycle Maintenance, after a lengthy odyssey to discover the meaning of "quality," concludes that "quality" exists in the striving for "arete," which is often translated from the Greek as "virtue" but which means "excellence." The odyssey was prompted by a student's asking Persig, a teacher of Rhetoric, if he taught

11

quality? Persig discovers that the much-maligned
Sophists (Rhetoricians), whom he defends against the
attacks of Plato and Aristotle, were teaching "excellence," the striving for excellence, which they held
up as a constant in any intellectual context. At the
ideal college the manifestations of this constant striving to achieve excellence will become a habit of thought
and action, the yardstick by which all ideas and projects are measured. Although compromise is desirable
in some contexts, here it is not. If a person were
observing a college community striving towards excellence, that person would discover a community constantly
agitated by ideas and proposals and projects. Execu-
tives at Kraft Foods say "a thought cannot be an idea
until it makes some people uncomfortable." The observer
would note that failure is compassionately accepted
as a necessary part of the striving process, but that
intellectual atrophy and academic inertia are the universally perceived enemies of the college. With regard
to the shared vision, then, "excellence" is doing well
what the college says it is doing.

Turner Revisited

Frederick Jackson Turner, as early as 1893, noted
that the Superintendent of the Census had announced
the closing of the American frontier in 1890. There
were no more horizons. It is only recently, however,
that the interstices along the frontier have been
so filled in that the fact of its closing has had an
impact on the minds and hearts of Americans. There
is now a broad consensus that there is no more room,
no undiscovered land waiting beyond the bourne of everyday experience to provide the promise of mystery --
just over the horizon. Turner says, "The appeal of
the undiscovered is strong in America." The observation
may be extended to include all humanity. The extraordinary development of America as a people, though,
has occurred because of the geographic largess of its
forever-unfolding frontier. Turner writes in his
masterpiece, The Frontier in America (1920), that
"the larger part of what has been distinctive and valuable in America's contribution to the history of the
human spirit has been due to the nation's peculiar
experience in expanding its type of frontier into new
regions." If this observation is correct -- and assum-
ing that America's "distinctive contribution" is worth
preserving and extending -- then the realities of the
present indicate that America will lose its distinctive
character if something is not done to provide new

frontiers. It is a principal thesis of this book that the educational community had better accept the challenge to discover and provide new frontiers. And the ideal liberal arts college will assuredly do so.

A recent commentator on the American scene noted that the present generation (1984) may very well be the first in the history of America which cannot expect to improve its material condition over that of its parents. Turner says that it is an American tradition "that each succeeding generation ought to find the Republic a better home." The "tradition" has been interpreted of late largely in materialistic terms. And the expectation of greater material gain did offer a frontier of sorts. Now, even that frontier may be closed. The possibility of the ocean or space providing frontiers for a very large number of people is remote. The globe becomes smaller and smaller. These observations will inspire the ideal college community to determine ways to provide a locus of dreams, a realm of expectation, a frontier for the insatiable yearnings of the human spirit which languishes and dies or suffers a metamorphosis into something hardly human if no horizon beckons. One might almost define homo sapiens as the primate that "longs for." Dante and Bunyan knew that each person is a homo viator, a person on a journey; and there is a psychological soundness beyond the themes of these great writers' works in viewing everyone as a wayfarer. The margins of experience -- until death -- must always fade forever into expectation.

What can the liberal arts college do to meet this challenge? It can offer a realm of values. The new frontier will be within, not without. Students must be made to discover within themselves the limitless frontiers of the mind and heart. They will be invited to internalize the quest for personal fulfillment (without becoming Narcissistic) by discovering a frontier of values which they can explore all along the wide borders of its possibilities. They will be encouraged to share their discoveries with others. The individualism that turns cancerous, such as that reported by Robert Bellah and others in their book, Habits of the Heart (1985), is prevented precisely because the object of the quest is values. Loyalty and a sense of commitment to others and not "psychological self-fulfillment" are the proper values of the old and new frontier. At the college described here, there exist in that new frontier vast landscapes that represent

13

all of human endeavor. The curriculum of the ideal
liberal arts college will describe these landscapes,
particularly in the traditional liberal arts courses,
but also throughout the entire curriculum -- a curriculum which has an added ingredient to whatever the concerns of the particular offering might be, namely,
a clearly defined context of values. The teachers at
this college will do what John W. Gardner (in his
speech, "Leading and Teaching," delivered to the Academy
of Educational Development) says that teachers must
do: ". . . teach the framework of values." Teachers
certainly will be responsible for the expertise demanded
of professors of a particular discipline or subject.
They will teach with dedication the arts and crafts
and ideas of their callings, but they will go beyond
that. They will lead their students to a vision of
new frontiers; they will, as Gardner says, "assert
a vision of what the society can be at its best."

Sixty-five years ago Turner summarized the character of the American people as resting on the three
"ideals" of "discovery, democracy, and individualism,"
and observed: "from the beginning of that long westward
march of the American people America has never been
the home of mere contented materialism." He saw
Americans, in other words, as a people with a vision
informed by specific values, carrying their ideas of
democracy and individual worth into the western frontiers; indeed, the vision was energetically realized
because of the frontier. The ideal liberal arts college
will "invoke" this Western spirit "for new and nobler
achievements."

The Personal Touch

Meaningful contact between all the personalities
that make up the college community is the sine qua
non that assures excellence as the mission and goals
of the shared vision are translated into action. The
observer will see ample evidence of the ways and means
employed to assure this contact. In the ideal college
being described here this program of meaningful contact
is the principal vehicle for realizing the ideal of
the shared vision. It is the type of the archetype,
the pragmatic imperative, the heart of the matter in
utilitarian terms of the everyday life of the college.
Any number of programs and policies derived from a
mission statement may be implemented in any number
of ways and may have relative success, but the ideal
implementation will not occur until there is pervasive

14

and genuine involvement by the individuals who make up the college community. A paradox emerges. Although involvement must be meaningful and broad, the hierarchical structures that inform the educational process and define the operation of the college must not be abandoned. Students must be involved closely with faculty, but the student-mentor relationship must be maintained. The faculty must be involved in policy making, but the administration must be independent in interpreting and implementing the policies of the college. The administration must be involved in the curriculum, but the faculty must ultimately determine its content. A "paradox" is a seeming contradiction, and there really is no contradiction in saying that within a hierarchical structure the value of individual participation is paramount. The ideal college will have this high level of meaningful contact which is advocated above without the individuals' in their various roles losing their identity. The student may work closely with a teacher on a research project, but both will know who is the student and who is the teacher. To be sure, all good teachers are devoted students and know that in the teacher-student relationship, the roles are likely to be reversed any number of times as the student inspires the teacher to learn and the teacher inspires the student to learn. This situation reflects the unselfish attitude of the true scholar who places ideas above self. Either end of the learning log will feel comfortable to the teacher or student. This reciprocity in learning is what one commentator calls the "flip-flop theory," and advocacy of this theory in no way detracts from the role of either the mentor or the student. The curators, administrators and faculty may become intellectual and social peers without blurring the lines of responsibility inherent in their separate roles. But the observer even here will note an added ingredient at the ideal college. As the Curators, administrators, faculty and students go about the business of their various tasks, they will not be concerned about territoriality; they will not worry about prerogatives. They will in fact exhibit a spirit of collegiality that will set the tone for learning and teaching and administering.

The Chronicle of Higher Education published in its October 24, 1984, issue the study of the select group of educators whose task was to report on "excellence in undergraduate education." The title of their report, "Involvement in Learning: Realizing the Potential of American Higher Education," signals the

15

principal theme of the report, namely, that meaningful contact is at the heart of effective learning:

> Many features of the teaching and learning environment in colleges and universities can be altered to yield greater student involvement in higher education. The fact that more learning occurs when students are actively engaged in the learning process has extensive implications for each faculty member and administrator in every institution. The most important implications of this fact can be stated in two fundamental principles about the conditions of educational excellence everywhere:
>
> 1. The amount of student learning and personal development associated with any educational program is directly proportional to the quality and quantity of student involvement in that program.
>
> 2. The effectiveness of any educational policy or practice is directly related to the capacity of that policy or practice to increase student involvement in learning.

At the ideal liberal arts college there will be ample evidence of specific programs that insure student involvement in all of the educational programs. The college catalog will reflect this emphasis. These programs will be explained in detail and bear the imprint of much planning and thought. They will not happen by chance. The number of programs will be limited to insure quality control. Each proposal to establish a program of "meaningful contact" will be greeted with enthusiasm but considered with caution. All proposals will be considered with reference to the academic mission and goals of the college and the curriculum in place to achieve those goals. That more learning goes on outside the classroom than in it is a common saw and, properly understood, no doubt true. Exchanges between students and faculty (and others) will occur outside the classroom in informal and incidental contexts, and these exchanges will often yield results far greater than those obtained in the classroom. Careful observers note, however, that these seeming incidental moments of inspiration and enlightenment were actually prepared for in the formal programs designed to assure that meaningful contact can indeed occur. Many an epiphany (to use Joyce's term broadly) outside the formal context had its genesis in a classroom or laboratory. This observation leads to a note of caution. The integrity of the traditional curriculum will be maintained at the ideal liberal arts college. The curriculum provides the intellectual grist for the mill of interaction. The deplorable reality of many ill-conceived and ill-executed non-traditional programs attempting to insure student participation is that the students do not have the vocabulary to participate. They must remain mute (or mouth inanities) because they do not have the background which comes from learning the fundamentals of any endeavor. They must not be contemptuous of rote memorization--although they will learn from some well-intentioned but poorly informed educators that rote memory work is useless or, somehow, stifles creativity. Pointless memory work done in a vacuum has limited value, but the Greeks were right in making Memory (Mnemosyne) the mother of the muses. Before student interaction can be meaningful, the students must have mastered a common body of information. Meaningful interaction between a faculty member and students focusing on a discussion of Hamlet can hardly occur if the students have not read and studied the play.

Mere indications that students meet with faculty, administrators, alumni, or others in contexts where contact is possible are not enough. Those long in the field who have become disenchanted with "innovative" programs which substitute gimmicks for substance, when hearing the words "student involvement" in relation to academic programs, understandably react negatively, equating "student involvement" with "rap" sessions and organized drivel. The quality of student involvement will receive as much attention as the types or quantity of programs, and there will be specific and detailed explanations of how this quality is determined (standards) and how this quality is part of the content of the program (method). Indeed, so important is the idea of student involvement in educational programs that all decisions and policies will be made in light of it. Most critically, decisions concerning the curriculum, personnel and budget will be made with the criterion of "student involvement" uppermost in the minds of the decision makers. And policies concerning extracurricular ("co-curricular" is the ideal term) activities will receive a revamping in that those responsible will begin to look for ways that student activities can be fitted into meaningful learning contexts. In order to achieve quality co-curricular programs, administrators will insure that a sustained dialogue between the faculty and the student affairs staff will occur. Should the observer discover such a dialogue, he will have come upon an extraordinary rarity in the groves of academe.

Meaningful contact between students and teachers will NOT be reserved principally for junior and senior students. A number of voices crying in the wilderness of the large state institutions have pointed out that freshman and sophomore students receive short shrift at these institutions. (Moreover, the entire undergraduate program is often, in practice if not in policy, considered as an afterthought. The graduate programs are the cynosure of every eye.) The "Involvement in Learning" report cited earlier recommends that "College administrators . . . reallocate faculty and other institutional resources toward increased service to first- and second-year students." In many courses, freshmen are taught by graduate assistants whose inexperience and dual role (teacher/degree candidate) definitely preclude "quality" student/teacher involvement. At some of the larger institutions, professors have been given freshman/sophomore classes to teach, but these assignments, for the most part, are viewed as odious. Oftentimes those who are not presently engaged in "significant" research receive these assignments. At the ideal college, publishing and teaching will not be mutually exclusive enterprises; but in any circumstance of daily academic life, the teaching and involvement with students must come first. And, most significantly, professors of all ranks will teach with conviction and zest on the freshman/sophomore level. These professors will not underestimate the intellectual capacities of their lower-level students, will not be condescending or aloof, and will create an "intense intellectual interaction between students and instructors," to quote again from "Involvement with Learning."

Finally, the degree (and hence the quality) of interaction between faculty and students is affected by the size of the institution where the interaction is to take place. Incompetent teachers and indifferent students may be found in small classes; the size of the class does not insure quality. Small class size (a favorable student-teacher ratio) is a necessary condition, however, to allow the best teaching and learning to take place. And the smallness must go beyond the classroom to the total learning environment,

the total size of the college. George Kuh in _Indices_
_of_ _Quality_ _in_ _the_ _Undergraduate_ _Experience_ says that
"quality appears to be mediated by the size of the
institution or the living-learning unit and by the
involvement on the part of students and faculty."
The first part of Kuh's sentence pertaining to the
size of the institution identifies the vehicle to
achieve the second part of the sentence pertaining
to the desired student-teacher involvement. A small
college provides the best setting for the best learning
to take place: if "personalization" is the touchstone
to realizing the ideal learning context, then a college
where the "living-learning unit" is the whole college
must be preferable to a large, impersonal university
necessarily fragmented because of the demands of size
and population.

Utile et Dulce

Any number of commentators on the current scene
in undergraduate education, most notably the panel
which wrote "Involvement in Learning: Realizing the
Potential of American Higher Education" (1984), have
pointed out the necessity "to restore liberal education
to its central role in undergraduate education." The
same panel notes that "the college curriculum has become
excessively vocational in its orientation." _At the_
ideal _liberal_ _arts_ _college_ _there_ _will_ _be_ _a_ _wedding_
_of_ _values_ _to_ _utility_. A common failing among American
colleges and universities is that they go about their
business in halves. These colleges and universities
are easily perceived metaphors for the either . . .
or fallacy. What is wanted is a college where the
ideal and the utilitarian are wedded equally in theory
and practice, _utile_ _et_ _dulce_. Even by the most secular
interpretation, people understand that they cannot
live by bread alone; but they also understand that
in this world they cannot live without it. An ideal
college will provide the setting for the development
of the physical and the spiritual, of both sides of
common human experience. Huston Smith, professor of
philosophy (Massachusetts Institute of Technology,
Syracuse) says, to paraphase loosely, that there are
three "absolutes" in human nature, the desire always
to have more, the desire to be whole, and the desire
to perceive mystery in existence. The ideal college
will speak to this triumvirate of desires in that the
"physical absolute" of the individual's wanting more
will be prepared for in the vocational and professional
aspect of the curriculum, the "philosophical absolute"

of the individual's desire for wholeness will be met in the liberal arts aspect of the curriculum, and both of these will be infused with the "spiritual absolute" of the desire for mystery in life in the system of values which governs and informs the whole life of the campus. The ideal college will not go about its business in halves: it will combine the liberal arts with the vocational and professional skills and arts, cementing the two with a clearly-defined system of values.

The Curriculum

The faculty at the ideal college will prescribe without apology a specific program of study in the liberal arts. The faculty will have the confidence to assert that its training and experience and shared vision make it the appropriate body to determine the specific curriculum for students. In the vocational and professional areas of the curriculum one seldom hears doubts about the propriety of the faculty's prescribing specific courses for specific vocations such as business administration or medicine. Much of the uncertainty concerning liberal arts or core requirements has come from faculties who have lost their vision and therefore their confidence. The absurdity of the laissez-faire curriculum is seen in the underlying assumption that the students know what is best for them. Students' desires and aspirations will obviously be considered and responded to genuinely, and there will be opportunities through electives in both the liberal arts part of the curriculum and the vocational and professional part to satisfy many of these desires. The choice of a major (area of concentration) remains solely with the students. But the determination of the corpus of knowledge and art and values which are representative of the common heritage of humankind, and more specifically, Western/American heritage, will be made by those responsible for its preservation, interpretation and dissemination--the college faculty. The danger in not prescribing a specific number of courses which "foster the shared values and knowledge that bind us together as a society" is that society is unbinding; it has disintegrated into political and social anarchy, a Babel of values, or worse, a society without values. The number of required courses in the liberal arts curriculum will reflect the conviction of the sentiments expressed above. A few courses scattered throughout the curriculum will not do. And the smorgasbord approach will not do.

The ideal college will have two full years (or close to it) of required liberal arts requirements, with the sciences, social sciences, fine arts and humanities well represented. And constant attention will be given by the teaching faculty to integrate the material from the general education segment of the curriculum with the material from the vocational/professional segment.

Although it is an end more to be hoped for than expected, at the ideal college all students would be required to study a modern language other than English. Certainly, all candidates for the Bachelor of Arts degree would be expected to meet a modern language requirement. Without becoming sanguine on the point -- and the temptation is great -- one could observe that the censure of the international community toward America's arrogant indifference toward other cultures and languages, the realization of America's ubiquitous international business and political involvement, and the necessity for all people to view this spaceship earth as a common carrier, certainly argue for a language requirement for all graduates of the ideal liberal arts college.

At the heart of this enterprise of teaching and learning, of gaining knowledge and wisdom, is the library. In "On Heroes and Hero Worship" Thomas Carlyle says that "if we think of it, all that a University, or final highest School can do for us, is still but . . . [to] teach us to read . . . The true University of these days is a Collection of Books." The library will not only be a collection of books, it will be the center of intellectual activity on campus, much frequented by the entire community of scholars. There will be evidence in the syllabuses of the overwhelming number of courses on campus that the work in the classroom goes beyond the textbook and that habits of creative and independent reading are nurtured. The inventory, the holdings, will not be the greatest concern; insuring student use will be. Obviously, the faculty and the librarians will do all they can with the resources available to assure that the holdings are current and sufficient to support the curriculum and the mission of the college. The librarians will think of themselves as teachers with the largest classroom on campus and be eager to help faculty and students to realize fully the resources of the library.

Liberal Arts and Liberal Learning

A distinction needs to be made between "liberal learning" and the "liberal arts." While the "liberal arts" aim at fostering the shared values and knowledge that bind a society together and at furnishing the individual student that dulce which makes life worthwhile, "liberal learning" is a more inclusive term and applies to all aspects of the college experience. It is, as John Henry, Cardinal Newman says, a "habit of mind . . . which lasts through life." The attributes are, according to Newman, "freedom, equitableness, calmness, moderation and wisdom." Of these characteristics of liberal learning, the two which enclose the rest in the quotation, "freedom" and "wisdom," are especially emphasized at the ideal college. "Freedom" is translated into providing education that allows the individual a multiety of opportunities in any context, the freedom that comes from being able to choose among possibilities rather than having to settle for no options. "Wisdom," that most elusive of terms, will be interpreted as the understanding that the sum of knowledge cannot be accounted for empirically.

Once the "habit of mind" Newman describes is pervasive throughout the campus -- and it will be at the ideal college -- there will be evidence of what some call an "intellectual atmosphere." Although the joie de vivre and high jinks that characterize the actions of college students will in no way be stultified by this intellectual atmosphere (who would want that?), the milieu of the campus will be one that can clearly be distinguished from, for instance, a high school. This atmosphere, much desired but widely absent on most college campuses, may not be legislated into existence through rules and regulations governing student life. The ferment of learning and seeking and finding and seeing feelingly (to paraphrase Gloucester in King Lear) will be such that students will be enamored of ideas and concerned with values and want to spend time thinking and acting on their ideas and values. The present will be so attractive that impatience with studies and programs and requirements that must be fulfilled to meet some future goals will vanish. The future will take care of itself.

The Future Is Now

Katherine Anne Porter in her book The Days Before (1952) recounts the following episode:

22

And as for the future, I was once reading the
first writings of a young girl, an apprentice
author, who was quite impatient to get on with
the business and find her way into print. There
is very little one can say of use in such matters,
but I advised her against haste -- she could so
easily regret it. "Give yourself time," I said,
"the future will take care of itself." This opin-
ionated young person looked down her little nose
at me and said, "The future is now." . . . maybe
she was right and the future does arrive every
day and it is all we have, from one second to
the next.

The account reflects both the impatience of young people
and their intuitive awareness of the importance of
the present. Their disdain of the future (and, assuredly, the past) is at once a mark of their immaturity
and a statement of their priorities. The faculty and
administration of the ideal college understand this;
that is to say, they understand young people. Great
pains will be taken to insure that the traditions and
lessons of the past will not be lost and that preparation for tomorrow will not be slighted. The penalties
for being ignorant of the past are severe and have
been amply commented upon, and a significant part of
the liberal arts program is devoted to making students
aware of their heritage, both the good and the bad.
And students understand, intellectually if not emotionally, that their studies are preparing them for tomorrow. Emotionally, although not philosophically it
is hoped, most students would agree with Jose Ortega
y Gasset that the here and now constitute reality:
". . . in the scale of realities 'lived' reality holds
a peculiar primacy" -- at least for young people.

An environment of learning and living that estab-
lishes that today is important will be clearly visible
at the ideal college. And the environment will be
good for everybody, not just the students. The daily
tasks of administrators, staff and faculty will take
on the vitality of the present, of the perception put
into practice that indeed the study of the past and
the hope of the future is for "the future that does
arrive every day." The lessons of the past are grand.
The future is vast. But the demands of the present
are immediate, often mundane, and usually readily iden-
tifiable. These demands of the present will be addressed in the policies and practices of the entire college
community; it will be understood that students need

to be accepted by their peers; that they need to experience success and failure without being overly im-
pressed with either; they they need to know, in other
words, that the college community is interested in
them now.   "Up Where We Belong," the popular theme
song from the movie, An Officer and a Gentlemen, has
the refrain, "All we have is here and now / All our
lives out there to find." The song reflects the attitude of the young.   In acknowledging the importance
of "here and now," the faculty and administration will
not be fostering hedonism or philosophic pessimism
or ignoring the lessons of the past or the hope of
the future.   The acknowledgement will be a simple
admission of the necessity of maintaining the vitality
that is peculiar to young people by subscribing to
the importance of today.

CHAPTER THREE

THE STUDENTS

"Our first wish is that all men should be educated
fully to full humanity; not only one individual,
nor a few, nor even many, but all men together
and single, young and old, rich and poor, of high
and low birth, men and women -- in a word, all
whose fate is to be born human beings . . . Our
second wish is that every man should be wholly
educated, rightly formed not only in one single
matter, or in a few, or even in many, but in all
things which perfect human nature."

Pampaedia by John Comenius

Dr. Samuel Johnson, the inimitable proponent of
common sense and clear thinking, when confronted with
overly large doses of speculation or theory, used to
boom out, "Put it to the test, Sir!" The burden of
the remaining chapters in this book is to provide specific examples of how the philosophy of Chapter Two may
be put into action. Providing specific programs of
ascertainable quality, defined by the touchstone of
personalization, governed by an explicit system of
values, and aimed at giving students freedom of choice
in all aspects of their lives is the raison d'être
of the ideal liberal arts college. All programs should
be measured by this yardstick. And all people, too.
Antecedent to all programs and the curriculum should
be faculty and administration which share this vision
by offering students their knowledge, their expertise,
their values, their dreams, their curriculum, and most
of all, their time.

Life-Stance

Before devising programs and curricula for students, the academy could well pause to remember what
it knows, or should know about students. And common
sense is called for here. The ideal faculty and administration know that students

(1) respond immediately to their feelings. "Now"
is important to students. A clearly-defined framework
of values, defended and practiced free of ambiguities
is of such immediate importance at an ideal liberal
arts college precisely because young people respond
primarily to the immediate. The challenge is clear.

Substance must be added to style. Students are surrounded with examples that teach that style is more important than substance. Money can buy happiness; so say the popular evening soap operas, the advertising industry, and any number of magazines which cater to young adults. But students soon become disillusioned in face of increasing drug use, the disintegration of the family, and spiritual boredom. The best lack all conviction, while the worst are full of passionate intensity. But education can change all that -- if the faculty understand young people. The faculty must understand that students not only need to know what they need, they must feel it.

(2) need constant motivation. It is hardly revelatory to say that motivation is a key to good teaching. And it is hardly newsworthy to report that a great many college students are bored with their courses. The solution to solving this academic ennui is simple but costly: a great deal of time in a personal context must be spent with students to match their immediate needs with what the faculty and administration are convinced are their long-range needs.

(3) need room to explore, fail or succeed, but in a framework of high expectations. Students need limits without boundaries. If one may understand the previous contradiction, one may go a long way towards understanding students. Students need criteria and guidelines and prescribed programs, but they also need the freedom to explore brave new worlds. Unnecessary roadblocks to exploration may be removed. For example, students who know that a high grade point average is requisite to gaining entrance to graduate or professional school may not attempt a course in Shakespeare if they feel a low grade might keep them out of advanced programs. Students should be allowed to take some courses outside of their major areas on a pass/fail basis, allowing them to explore new horizons without fear.

(4) need praise. So universal is this characteristic of human nature one wonders why it does not receive more attention on college campuses. Because of this need for praise, peers assert a disproportional influence. Student behavior often changes dramatically because of the influence of peers. New adult mentors play an important role in the young person's experiments. The setting, therefore, becomes of paramount importance as students respond to people in a new

environment. Social organizations, class activities, co-curricular activities in music, drama or sports -- all furnish "locales" where praise may be earned by students. If these activities are closely monitored and bear the imprint of a clear-cut system of values, they will have a lasting positive influence on students. And students need praise in their classes.

(5) want mentors who are not peers. Students want faculty to be faculty, not peers or buddies. The academy has known this for a long time but lost its nerve and its direction when "intellectual authority came to be replaced by intellectual relativism as a guiding principle of the curriculum," as William J. Bennett observes. A number of professors have given up their authority to become chums with students, a "cop out" to use the vernacular of the students, that breeds indifference and mistrust in the students. Respect for the subject and the professor of the subject are necessary for the best learning to take place.

(6) expect faculty to demand high performance. Of course, students expect tolerance for errors and they expect faculty to understand that learning involves failures, but they also expect criteria for performance that makes their completion of the task or a course or a degree worthwhile and broadly recognized as such.

(7) know grades are important. Once one has acknowledged that grades are merely a means to an end, not the end itself, he may observe that students know by everything they have heard or seen that grades are important: their credits, degrees, transcripts, entrance requirements to graduate or professional schools, academic honors, parental and public approval, and so forth all tell them that grades are indeed important. Grades should indicate learning is taking place. And an academic support system should be in place (see below) which demonstrates to students that the faculty and administration know grades are important.

(8) must be taken seriously. The accidental advantage of age and experience on the part of faculty and administrators should not result in indifference, condescension or superiority. Students are to be taken seriously, and the approach is to involve them meaningfully in the learning process. And personal problems are to be taken seriously, too.

(9) perform best in a personalized context.

27

The thrust of a good part of this book demonstrates that without a high degree of personalization, a consistently high degree of learning will not take place.

Further observations of students through the lens of common sense reveal that students are creatures with seemingly boundless energy who enliven any context through their constant agitation as they struggle with the paradox which defines them. Students are walking paradoxes. They are at once pragmatic and idealistic. They grow impatient with the wisdom that counsels patience and future rewards, but talk constantly of the ways things "ought" to be. They resent authority but perish without it. They are tolerant with faculty and each other so long as they do not feel cheated or duped. They are disproportionately influenced by peers. They seek mentors and are susceptible to unscrupulous gurus. And the total environment where they study is directly related to their behavior: a value-oriented setting where caring adults take the time to be personal while holding up high codes of conduct and academic standards is the environment students thrive in. In fact, it is ideal.

And somebody has to harness all this energy called students and give it direction. This is the "bedrock" of the faculty's mission. The type of symbiosis in nature where mutual benefits derive from a relationship could serve as an analogy for the relationship between students and faculty. The faculty provides the substance in the relationship and the students the life. This symbiotic "life-stance" is easily perceived, because students are the life of the campus, actually and metaphorically. And the faculty are assembled to give meaning and substance and--assuredly--direction to that life. When the metaphor is best realized, the campus will be alive with intellectual and artistic motion as the faculty works to feed and satisfy the creative energies of the students. And this energy enlivens and sustains the faculty who are inspired to meet the challenge of the students. Symbiosis cannot occur when there is too great a distance between organisms, between the mutually benefiting entities-- and that is the reason why the "conversational context" is so important. That is also the reason "personalization" should be the touchstone of the whole educational enterprise.

Almost everyone knows, even a bachelor of arts, that colleges admit students, advise students, teach

28

students, grade students and graduate students. Most colleges house students, monitor activities, offer financial aid and counseling services, and provide recreational centers and food services. Colleges identify their constituencies, court their alumni and friends, and raise money (usually in that order). Most have boards of trustees, top-heavy administration, and faculty with problems concerning salaries, benefits and tenure. But there will be a difference at the ideal college, and the difference is the touchstone against which all of the activities and services and learning and teaching and management mentioned above are measured -- <u>personalization</u>. When a student asks an obviously busy faculty member, "Can I see you?" the only answer is "yes," even if it means arranging for a later conference. The immediate personal response -- even of a brief duration--adds the personal touch. Scholarships are common, but when personalization is the touchstone, scholarship recipients communicate with the donors on a regular basis. This emphasis on personalization, which obviously requires a great expenditure of time on the part of the faculty, has been criticized by some as coddling students, of robbing them of their chance to become independent, and, when applied to the classroom, of spoon-feeding them. The ideal college rejects this criticism as a self-serving rationalization to avoid spending time with students. A great deal of attention can be given students, especially freshmen students, without deterring their inevitable push towards independence. <u>So long as standards are set to assure excellence and "quality" is the principal subject in all courses, the so-called "spoon-feeding" will easily be seen as nothing more than highly personalized instruction.</u> Fledglings who become too dependent on a mentor can be pushed from the next--and that is a personal response, too.

Two highly structured programs are offered here to insure that "personalization" is more than a slogan to soothe anxious parents, that "quality" is pervasive, and that "programs" prepare students to "be wholly educated . . . in all things which perfect human nature."

I.

A Paradigm for Personalization

With the exception of colleges with open admission policies or those with decidedly lax entrance requirements, it is assured that students who are admitted

to liberal arts colleges in America are capable of
doing the academic work required. Each year, however,
nearly one-third of the freshman classes fail to meet
a minimum grade point average. Obviously, the dictum
that "high admission standards guarantee high performance " just isn't sound. Having high standards for
admission is just a beginning (a necessary one) for
the college striving for excellence. What happens
to the student who performs well in high school but
falls by the academic wayside in college? The answer,
while involved, is at the same time simple: the student
has substituted priorities and lost--the student might
say "escaped"--a parental monitoring system. The
student may express more freely resistance to authority,
explore new-found freedoms, and suffer some trauma
in discovering that classes are considerably more difficult than those in high school. The student may just
decide not to attend class simply because there is
a choice. At the ideal liberal arts college, a thorough
academic support system will be developed to respond
to students who need help in maintaining priorities
and to students who need challenges beyond the expected.
Some students enter college in need of immediate
academic support beyond that provided in the established
program of instruction. Others enter with talents
and energies that demand another type of support, a
program for high fliers. Most students fall somewhere
in between these two groups (moving up and down between
them at some time during their careers) and must not,
as often happens, be excluded from the process of
personalizing because they are taken for granted.
The "Paradigm for Personalization" accounts for every
student enrolled, regardless of talents or level of
performance.

Academic Monitoring: A Bold and Certainly Not Modest Proposal

The following proposal outlining an ideal academic
monitoring system is costly in time and money, but
it is ultimately "cost effective" in two ways: (1)
it provides an effective method of personalizing teaching and learning and (2) it increases the rate of
student retention. Every student should be assigned
to a full-time faculty member who serves as the student's academic advisor. Students may change advisors
if they choose. Insofar as possible students should
be matched with advisors in their field of study or
areas of special interest. The faculty advisory system
serves as the basis for the monitoring of the academic

life of every student. In terms of the paradigm above, the greater number of students, those who matriculate at the "B" or "C" level of performance, are challenged by consistently high academic standards and a demanding curriculum. They graduate with the knowledge that their degree has meaning. Their teachers and advisors constantly hold before them possibilities of higher achievement, and their peers who are the high achievers beckon them with their performance. Some do move to a faster track (and some to a slower), but those who do not or cannot move up have nonetheless mastered a program of study of which they can be proud. The "B" and "C" level students are usually well adjusted and take advantage of the social and co-curricular activities offered by the college. They have a pretty clear idea of where they are going and how they are going to get there. The academic monitoring system should keep a steady eye on this group which accounts for the greatest number in the student body.

Probationary Students. It appears that the under-achievers or academically deficient students get the most attention in the model being outlined, and in terms of hours of contact between these students and faculty and support staff, they do. In terms of programs provided and opportunities afforded, they do not. The students who enter the paradigm at the probationary level should be monitored weekly, with each instructor who has the students in class reporting on their progress (or lack of it) to the academic dean. They should be assigned to spend eight to ten hours of study at the Student Development Center each week, and their performance there should be reported to the academic dean weekly. The probationary student should also arrange for weekly meetings with his advisor. The academic dean, the probationary student's advisor, the student's teachers, and the staff of the Student Development Center all should be monitoring the performance of the student admitted on probation and assessing his performance weekly. If the probationary student does not achieve a grade point average above the academic probationary level by the end of the first semester, the student should not be allowed to return.

Monitoring Class Performance: An Early Warning System. At the end of the first four weeks of classes of every semester, the faculty should submit to the academic dean (with copies to the advisors) the names of all students who have grades of "D" or "F". (Monitoring this early in the semester, by the way, is virtually nonexistent in higher education.) From the initial reporting, at least <u>four</u> personal contacts will be assured: the academic dean sees the student, the advisor sees the student, the staff of the Student Development Center sees the student, and the teacher who reported the "D" or "F" sees the student. A great many students who find the transition from high school to college difficult or who are academically weak or who simply get behind will be rescued from failure because of this early warning system. The same procedure as outlined above should be repeated at mid-term. By mid-term, in other words, a student who is performing below average will have had at least eight programmed and required meetings with the whole array of academics responsible for the student's progress, from the academic dean to the student's instructors.

Students expect and want academic monitoring, but they resist "parenting". The monitoring system outlined above is one way to translate "caring" into a personalized approach to education. Students will understand that their teachers really care about their performance, about D's and F's. And through these personal contacts, problems or concerns other than academic ones (but ones which inhibit learning) are discovered and addressed. Support for the student in all areas of human behavior or activity becomes possible; this early-warning system makes personalization possible, practical, and effective.

<u>High Fliers</u>. For those students who consistently perform at a high level of achievement, the Academic Monitoring Program exists primarily to provide opportunities and offer challenges. Joseph Wood Krutch once observed that in many instances, education in America, attempting to realize the Jeffersonian ideal of educating everyone, instead reduced education to the "lowest common denominator". A college need not abandon the dream of the democratic ideal in order to have standards and in order to provide the limitless opportunities on which the achievers thrive. The standards at the ideal liberal arts college will be such that they may be broadly recognized, and the definition of excellence by which programs are judged will not be formulated from local standards only. "Excellence" therefore, may be defined as "the state of possessing good qualities in an unusual or eminent degree as measured by standards widely accepted." The <u>recognized</u> presence of a group of high achievers adds color to the academic setting, without which a common grayness covers every-

thing. An osmotic process of increasing excellence inevitably takes place as the high achievers pull up all below, thereby raising standards and expectations.

The high fliers should be provided with opportunities which allow them to soar beyond the middle flight as they pursue things formerly unattempted. If nothing else, the administration and faculty should work creatively not to get in the way of these high achievers. At the outset, those who can and want to go beyond the expected are identified. A number of academic scholarships, of course, should be awarded to these and other students of merit. Advisors should acquaint their students with the possibility of acquiring scholarships for current and future study. A Scholarship Committee, whose primary responsibility is to help students secure scholarships and fellowships, should be in place to work closely with the academic dean and the students' advisors. And the honors program should include freshmen as well as juniors and seniors, with designated "honors courses" for all high fliers and special "honors colloquia" for advanced students.

One of the most noteworthy programs that could be provided for the high fliers is an Alumni Preceptors Program--a program which provides opportunities for students to study in situ in their chosen fields of interest with alumni who are recognized for their accomplishments in a particular field. For example, pre-medical students might be placed with medical doctors who are alumni, pre-law students with lawyers who are alumni, and business students with recognized leaders in business who are alumni. Those on the "A" track (and above) should be given fellowships that allow them to work closely with professors on special research projects. And, allowances for the high achievers should be made in individual courses. Syllabuses should not be so rigid that an individual response to a student's talents and performance is precluded. The theatre, the athletic fields, the art studio and the music hall offer additional opportunities for the high achievers to soar as high as their talents and energies will take them.

An extraordinary amount of time is spent monitoring the academic progress of students, but the philosophy which should guide all programs insists that just such involvement with students is the very place where time and energies should be spent.

The Curriculum

The curriculum is the foundation on which the Paradigm for Personalization rests. And any curriculum is only as good as its faculty. Jacques Barzun in _Teacher in America_ (1945, 1981) describes the sadness of the college or university where teachers do not teach, and adds, "The duty to teach well cannot be legislated." Of course, he is correct. But good teaching can be assured by identifying, securing or maintaining, and rewarding those who subscribe to the idea that a teacher's place is with students and providing them contexts for meaningful involvement with their students. Assembling such a faculty is not easy since making judgments is involved, and the college or university of today will do a great deal to avoid making judgments about teaching performance; but the paralysis of will attendant to the process of assessing and evaluating professors, pervasive throughout higher education, must be overcome. The faculty should know its mission, its worth, its pre-eminent role in formulating the curriculum and educating its students, and further that it has a context of absolute academic freedom. In addition, it must have a sense of community in its shared vision.

The curriculum at the liberal arts college ought to emphasize the liberal arts, obviously. At least 48-60 hours of specific course work should be required of all students graduating with a bachelor's degree. A minimum of two semesters of study in a foreign language should be required of _all_ graduates, but in this imperfect world the compromise is to have such a requirement for BA students only. Transfer students, regardless of the hours in composition taken elsewhere, should be required to pass a proficiency examination prepared and graded by the members of the English department. Transfer students who fail to pass the proficiency examination should be required to pass the advanced composition class before being allowed to graduate. This type of quality control is rare but will indicate the emphasis placed on program quality and writing skills in the curriculum at the ideal college.

Those required courses which "foster the shared values and knowledge that bind us together as a society" should come from all departments of learning, defined under the traditional categories of arts, social sciences, humanities, and science. The specificity of the liberal arts requirement in depth and breadth is an index of the confidence of the faculty in its vision and in its ability to prescribe a program of study. There are no smorgasbord offerings in the model proposed here. The faculty should aim at achieving significant integration of the general education part of the curriculum with courses from the major field of study. Guest lectures by fellow faculty, cross referencing of current syllabuses, special lecture series, special programs, etc., are ways to achieve this end.

Within each discipline, habits of independent study should be encouraged as students are taught the particular "vocabulary" of the discipline. Although each discipline has its minimal content which it is obligated to incorporate into its program of study, the critical skills, problems and lore unique to the particular study should be emphasized equally with content. In fact, one finds it amusing to observe some curricula with a seemingly inexhaustible array of courses -- from Piscatory Eclogues of The Seventeenth Century to The Psychology of Parlor Games. A multiplicity of courses does not serve as a substitute for good teaching and student involvement.

II.

Triad of Quality

Having a good curiculum in place interpreted by teachers in courses whose principal subject is quality, is assumed but not taken for granted at the ideal college. Beyond that the world, in its infinite variety of people, ideas and places, is also the classroom for the properly oriented student. Assuring that students keep in contact with this larger classroom and its broad curriculum is the business of the liberal arts college. Practically, this requires that specific measures be taken to insure that all students have opportunities to travel and study off campus and that the ideas and art and personalities beyond the campus are brought to the campus. Study off campus and an active convocation program are especially important for students in colleges which are geographically isolated. Even more, a context must be provided to insure that the highest return possible results from the study abroad and the programs brought to campus --and that what is learned is integrated with the formal curriculum. Experience and hard data have

35

shown (See Chapter Two) that the more involvement students have in the learning process and with their mentors and fellow students, the more they learn. And common sense, if not studies like those by George D. Kuh (cited earlier), show that the smaller the class size, the more learning takes place. But even at a college with an academically desirable student-teacher ratio, uniformity of class size and total student part-ticipation are not guaranteed. It is necessary, there-fore, to superimpose a structure on the traditional framework of classes to insure that every student can get in on the conversation.

Study Abroad

Study off-campus (study abroad) has always been viewed as educationally desirable -- for those who can afford it. The "grand tour" once formed the cap-stone of the college careers of privileged Americans and Europeans. But very few students can or do travel abroad, largely for two reasons: they can't afford it or they simply see no reason to. A great many students at liberal arts colleges receive financial aid and simply cannot, on their own, afford to partici-pate in off-campus programs. Too, a great many students are highly parochial whether they are from a college located in a city or a remote village, with attitudes and tastes to match their limited backgrounds. Fully believing with Mark Twain that "travel is fatal to prejudice, bigotry and narrow-mindedness" and that "broad, wholesome, charitable views of men and things cannot be acquired by vegetating in our little corner of the earth all one's lifetime," the ideal college will develop a program which allows all students to enroll to study off-campus. This action will indicate that the ideal college is interested in educating students in a program of excellence regardless of their financial status.

A Suggested Program: Janaway. The following program for off-campus study is in place and thriving at a small, private liberal arts college in the Midwest.

It has been praised by the Academy for Educational Development in its publication, The Idea Handbook for Colleges and Universities, as one of the most innovative and outstanding offerings in higher education. It is offered here as an ideal model to insure that students have an opportunity to study beyond the campus. The faculty devised the study-abroad program as part of the formal curriculum. The academic calendar has been arranged so that between the first and second semesters there is an interim period during the month of January. During this interim period no courses are offered on campus; all courses are offered away from campus for a two-or three-week period, hence the name of the program--Janaway. During the school year preceding the study abroad, the faculty and students determine the location and content for a course, incorporate their findings into a course syllabus and proposal, and submit the proposal (with syllabus) to the department chairperson and the academic dean for approval. The academic dean assures that duplication does not occur, that logistical matters are well considered, and that the program of study is sound academically. There is no attempt, however, to equate the content or purpose of the two- or three-week programs abroad with the strictly academic offerings in the curriculum. The two hours of credit given for each course may not be used to meet either distribution (general education) or concentration (major area of study) requirements. The faculty and administration are convinced, however, of the worth of these offerings and believe it would be a narrow view of education, indeed, to deny travel and study abroad as part of a sound liberal arts program.

Such programs cost money and there must be a genuine commitment on the part of the faculty, administration, and curators that off-campus study is a highly desirable part of the curriculum. The college community must want such a program as Janaway to succeed. And Janaway has been successful at its parent college. The first complement of courses was offered in January, 1979. Since then, courses have been offered in England and Wales; Old Mexico; Greece and Turkey; Quebec; San Francisco; New York City; Washington, D.C.; and the Florida Keys. (San Francisco and New York City are as remote from the experiences of most college students in the Midwest as Turkey is.) The particulars of the program are these: the college provides housing, meals, and a travel allowance for all Janaway participants. Tuition is free to all full-time students. Janaway courses are taught by full-time faculty. Students pay a course fee to cover on-site travel (and for the courses in Europe, to supplement travel allowance), and laboratory costs (tickets to required plays, concerts, lectures, historical sites, museums, etc.). Spending money is the responsibility of the students.

The program _per se_ is innovative and deserving of its accolades, but the success of Janaway has resulted from careful planning and commitment to a shared vision on the part of the faculty. The key to the program's success has been the intensity of involvement between faculty and students and the highly orchestrated itinerary which fills the students' days and evenings with worthwhile things to do.

The inspiration and enthusiasm that result from these off-campus experiences can hardly be measured. Of course, the instructors benefit equally (if not more so) from the opportunities to see and hear and taste and smell and touch what heretofore had been reserved for the senses of the mind. The classes in biology and history and literature (etc.) come alive as students identify with the lessons to be learned. But even more, specific information is gained from libraries, museums, performances, historical sites, and so forth. For example, a political science major studying the separatist movement in Quebec, Canada, spent two weeks in 1979 interviewing leaders of the movement and collecting pertinent data. Literature majors have followed specific itineraries focusing on the life and works of a particular author. And the list goes on. But perhaps the most important benefit of all is the relationship that develops between faculty and students. Continual contact for two or three weeks, virtually twenty-four hours a day, can build a mentor-student relationship unparalleled in the usual academic context. Over a four-year period, the percentage of students who will have the opportunities to form such a relationship is significant.

The Convocation Program

Almost all colleges have a convocation program. Few take full advantage of such a program as a vehicle to (1) extend learning beyond the classroom, and (2) develop a "conversational context" (i.e., greater interaction between faculty and students). J. B. Priestly in _Thoughts in the Wilderness_ (1957) warns of "block" thinking, the uncritical adoption of some particular point of view, the wholesale purchase of a "neat set of beliefs and opinions". At the heart of this essay, although he does not say it, is the disdain for thinkers who are emotionally and intellectually prisoners of the either . . . or fallacy; and, more simply, his disdain for those who have closed minds. The inability to see beyond two possibilities into the complexities of the modern world has resulted, thinks Priestly, in the inaction and indecision characteristic of the overwhelming number of people and institutions. Colleges and universities attempt, or should attempt, to assemble a faculty and administration (although it is rare among administrations) with different backgrounds, expertise, beliefs and personalities. This assembly of many points of view in no way contradicts the earlier assertion that the greater number of those assembled must share their vision of what the college is to be and do. The belief in the mission and goals of an enterprise of learning (the shared vision), properly understood (i.e., where the free investigation and exchange of ideas is jealously guarded), invites diversity of opinion and experience. Genuinely and critically exploring any number of possibilities certainly does not mean that one should not adopt a particular point of view. Harold McMillan, sometime Prime Minister of England, tells the story of his valedictory meeting with a respected professor. He discovered the professor buried behind a desk of papers and books and announced that he was there to say farewell. The professor, without ceremony, asked, "What have you learned?" The young Harold McMillan haltingly replied, "I have learned to look at both sides of an issue." To which the professor responded: "I trust you've learned to come down on one side or the other." At the ideal liberal arts college, a context for looking at all sides of an issue will be provided within a framework of values and critical thinking, a context where scrutiny of many points of view does not preclude action.

The off-campus study program discussed above is one way the students at the ideal college are exposed to new ideas. The college, as it were, takes the students to the ideas. The convocation program, on the other hand, brings the ideas to the students. A carefully administered, creatively selected, adequately funded, and academically integrated convocation program is an invaluable means of supplementing the diversity of opinion that exists, hopefully, among the faculty. A selection of ideas, art, personalities, attitudes, prejudices and skills for the students (and the entire college community) to respond to is provided by such a program. The logistics must be such that the convocations will be at times when all students can attend and the academic policy must be such that all will attend.

An added ingredient to insure that students will indeed profit from the bringing of ideas, art and personalities to campus would be a system which would allow absolute student participation, a system of organizing students into small groups which are required to respond to the convocation programs in an organized way, but a way that will insure the "conversation context."

The Conversation Context

If, as stated earlier, personalization of the learning experience is the touchstone of quality in learning, then providing a setting for that high degree of student-faculty interaction to take place is mandated. This desired setting can be accomplished in two ways: (1) In all programs in and out of the formal curriculum, time spent with students should be advanced by the administration as the summum bonum; informally -- but not incidentally -- professors should meet regularly with their students in the halls and in their homes. (2) Beyond the universally practiced but un-programmed emphasis on student-teacher interaction should be a formal program of grouping students into pods of ten or fifteen students, each directed by a faculty member. The groups should not be considered as classes, and pains should be taken to avoid the classroom atmosphere of teachers giving and students receiving. In fact, the group sessions should be planned to provide students with a conversational context, a learning situation divorced from the formality and inhibitions often associated with the classroom. The syllabus for each group might be, largely, the convocation programs. The students in each group would attend the convocation programs with their mentors and then meet immediately after the convocation for a discussion and assessment of the program. A one-page essay might be required for all students, written towards the end of the discussion period, which represents the students' ideas and their abilities to synthesize and organize their ideas economically and spontaneously. And attention must be given to format and standards of usage in the writing.

Although the convocation program will provide a certain uniformity of interest (the basic content for the group discussions), each group will have a personality of its own. The groups will be formed as students elect to join professors who have formulated and published a proposal outlining a particular focus

40

of interest for the group. The possibilities will
reflect not only the different academic areas in the
curriculum, but also particular interdisciplinary
interests on the part of the professors. Once formed,
groups may elect to attend off-campus programs at neigh-
boring colleges and universities, adopt a reading list
for the group, attend specific campus functions other
than the convocation programs (and this is encouraged),
and any number of things that suit the interests of
the groups. In addition, each year the faculty could
adopt a common reading for the entire campus, and ideas
from the reading might appear as motifs throughout
the intellectual life of the campus. The groups would
read and respond to the reading and the ideas generated
by the entire campus community. This common reading
would add one more item for discussion which would
be common to all groups.

Finally, the discussion groups are to be viewed
as supplementing and clarifying the curriculum. In
fact, these groups should be viewed as one way to
achieve the goals of the curriculum which, certainly,
must be the solid foundation on which all of the programs outlined above are built.

Suggestions for a Program for Success

1. Adopt as a pre-eminent criterion in measuring
faculty effectiveness the time faculty spend with
students; i.e., the relative level of "personalization
of instruction." Faculty appointments, promotions,
salary increases, and tenure should all be considered
in terms of this criterion.

2. Adopt a "life-stance" model for the student-faculty
relationship; i.e., develop a model to encourage a
symbiotic relationship between students and faculty
based on personalization of instruction and clear iden-
tification of the respective roles and motives of
students and faculty.

3. Adopt a "paradigm" for personalization; i.e., an
academic monitoring and support system based on identifying levels of student performance and responding
with clearly-developed programs to personalize the
monitoring and supporting. It is imperative to include
an "early warning system" in the paradigm.

4. Adopt a liberal arts requirement for the curriculum
that is specific, thorough (48-60 hrs.), and traditional

in its representation from the sciences, social sciences, arts and humanities.

5. Adopt a program to insure quality of instruction through increased levels of personalization of instruction, and through programs such as subsidized off-campus or study-abroad courses, convocation programs integrated into the curriculum, and the creation of groups or pods of students under a faculty mentor to establish the most favorable "living-learning unit."

CHAPTER FOUR

THE FACULTY AND THE ACADEMY

"And gladly would he learn, and gladly teach."

Geoffrey Chaucer

Melampus, perhaps the first great seer in Greek mythology, had the special gift of being able to understand what birds and animals said to each other. Being imprisoned after failing in one of his adventures, he earned his release by eavesdropping on worms gnawing the roof beams where he was imprisoned, learning from the worms' conversation that the structure was to collapse the next day at dawn. Taking advantage of his special gift, he alerted his captors, escaped the collapse, and was rewarded for giving the warning. The faculties of liberal arts colleges need to attune their ears to the worms gnawing away at the structure of undergraduate education. They don't even need to know what the worms are saying, but they had better identify the species and apply a pesticide (organic, of course). Indifference to teaching is eating away the integrity of undergraduate programs. The problem in most instances is not that teachers cannot teach. It is simply that they will not teach (or will not teach to an acceptable degree of performance) or that they are in contexts that will not allow them to teach. The vastly greater number fall in the latter category. To shore up the worm-eaten structure of undergraduate education, faculty and administrators must focus their attention on redefining the scholarship which must inform teaching. And first off, faculty need to understand some things about themselves.

Faculty Profile

In terms of the larger mission and the general welfare of the whole college, faculty are often myopic. The concerns of their special disciplines, which must hold a certain primacy in their thoughts and actions, make it difficult for them to see beyond special interests or departmentalized concerns. The mission and goals of the college are often approached from any number of viewpoints. At the ideal college the shared vision of what the college as a whole is and should be supersedes localized concerns. Faculty members are trained to think rationally and objectively and will focus their eyes on universal concerns if

43

a context is present for them to do so. If faculty do not share the vision of what the definition of the college is, no "edict" or administrative maneuvering will be--in the long run--successful. Faculty can "study" proposals to death. They can debate cogently and arrive at nothing. They can go underground, both politically, and intellectually. The college president and his academic administrators must provide the vehicle (see Chapter Five) to achieve the singleness of purpose for faculty which allows each faculty member and each department to fit the concerns of each into the larger framework.

One common misconception about college teachers is that they are gregarious, that they like to be with students. It is assumed that since they find lecturing the easiest form of breathing, they must enjoy talking with students. Although there are notable exceptions, the greater number of college teachers, left to their own inclinations and to the definition of scholarship and the system of rewards which guide their teaching, would rather be in the library or in their studies at home than with students. The pattern of training experienced in graduate school does little to encourage the Ph.D. candidate to spend time with students. Teaching and laboratory assistants endure their teaching assignments with Grecian fortitude as part of the suffering expected in the acquisition of knowledge. They graduate into the ranks of college professors correct in their assumption that they will not be rewarded for spending time with students, but for publishing or reading a paper at a conference or serving as a member of a, hopefully, "prestigious" study group.

Personalized Teaching

Those skills associated with successful interpersonal communication are often neglected or scoffed at. The reciprocal benefits of the "flip-flop theory" discussed in Chapter Two are overlooked. The solution is to redefine the role of the undergraduate faculty, stressing the central importance of time spent with students and rewarding faculty for creative teaching. One of the greatest contributions an administrator can make to learning is getting students and faculty together in a "conversational context." Once again, an either . . . or fallacy need not be committed: good teaching will undoubtedly restrict the volume of publishing (an additional boon to scholarship since so much that is written is remote or repetitious),

<u>but</u> <u>it</u> <u>will</u> <u>not</u> <u>restrict</u> <u>scholarship</u>. Faculty must demonstrate their scholarship and be rewarded for that scholarship, but "scholarship" must be redefined. A paper written from some obscure corner of knowledge and published in an "acceptable" journal, although valued as an end in itself, is <u>not</u> valued nearly so much as evidehce of teachers' keeping current in their fields and translating that currency to the classroom. And contexts should be provided so that scholarship can be shared with students outside the laboratory or classroom (see Chapter Three).

The process of scholarship and the rewards that derive from scholarship need to be experienced by the student as well as the teacher. This goal can be achieved by the programmed "conversational context." Professors must be made aware that they will be rewarded for time spent with students outside the classroom. Teachers who are demonstrably current in their fields of interest and who are demonstrably good teachers will be held up as role models. But beyond that, there should be programs which do not leave to chance the personalization of the learning process. The Janaway program discussed in Chapter Three allows students two or three weeks in an unfamiliar setting to share ideas and experiences with faculty. The "pod" program, assembling students in groups of ten or so for special study with a mentor who is a full-time professor, is another way to make sure that the scholarship done by the professoriate reaches the most important audience (also discussed in Chapter Three). Following the graduate model, the ideal college might develop a program to allow upper-level students of high academic achievement to work as fellows or "departmental scholars" with faculty of their choice. The students who desire to participate in this highly competitive program would be selected by an academic department. The possibilities of specific activities vary widely. For example, some of these students might work as research assistants in the library or the laboratory. Some might work as tutors in the Student Development Center. Some might work off-campus in business or government or private laboratories as interns. All of these students, in whatever context, should work closely with a faculty mentor. They should be significantly involved in each project both quantitatively and qualitatively. They should not be mere academic lackeys. The "conversational context" will not work if the faculty and students have nothing to converse about. Scholarship misses its principal consumer--from the point of view advanced here--if that scholarship involves only an exchange between faculty peers in a journal or at a meeting of a learned society. The aim is to make the process whole, to join rigorous scholarship to vigorous teaching. And to do so, the old approaches have been modified, transmuted by the touchstone of personalization.

Faculty Rewards

Faculty need rewards which support and reinforce the ideal teacher/scholar model outlined above. The spiritual, intellectual and aesthetic rewards derived from pursuing knowledge as its own end, although powerful and prime motivators, are not enough. The rewards which derive from students' being metamorphosed from simple organisms into thinking and feeling human beings, although peculiarly satisfying to teachers, are not enough. The imprint of a pat on the back or the sweet sounds of praise are ephemeral. All are important, but none is sufficient. What is needed is money. Money alone is not enough, of course, since the word "ideal" figures prominently in these essays, but without it, all else fails. If administrators and faculty are honest enough to leave the pure ether of "higher" motivations, they will admit that genteel penury, however intellectually endowed, is not ideal. Faculty and administrators should not be deluded into thinking that the Euclidian bare beauty of the intellect in action will substitute for adequate salaries or realistic benefits. And since faculty, for the most part, take their cues from the academic dean and the president and since these two administrators exert the principal influence at the small, liberal arts college, they must demonstrate the leadership to be clear in what they expect and certain in their system of rewards. And these matters are too important to be left to personalities or to chance. A thorough professional assessment and development program, therefore, is fundamental to the passing out of the money.

The Professional Development Program

The ideal approach to faculty professional development is to match the college's available resources for such purposes with the professional aspirations of each faculty member. Such a process is time-consuming and requires administrators who are willing to respond to each faculty member personally. Once again, "personalization" is central to the process.

There must be parameters of possibility, obviously: the faculty member's aspirations must fit within the mission and goals of the college and the expectations of the faculty member's discipline. What is unique in the model proposed here is not the array of possibilities for professional faculty development--travel, sabbaticals, workshops, conferences, research grants, released time, etc. What is unique is the personal approach. And the personal approach requires generous expenditures of that most precious of commodities, time. Too, there must be a vehicle within the context of personalization to assure the legitimacy, the integrity, of the professional development program. The way is to relate the aims of the faculty member and the aims of the college to the discipline that gives the faculty member a professional identity. In this instance, it is psychologically and administratively sound to move from the particular to the general. It is far easier for faculty members to see how they relate to their disciplines than how they relate to problems of declining enrollment or increased costs for faculty insurance.

Evaluation of Faculty Performance

The particulars of the development program become more explicit as they are converted to standards of judgment by which salaries, promotions, tenure, etc., are considered. Ideally, faculty members would organize a development plan which would itself be used in the evaluation process, a process which must always be on-going. Ambiguities and uncertainties arise if the professional development plan is divorced from the judgments which affect faculty in such telling ways. The idea (the plan) is only realized in action (how the faculty member performs). If a faculty member is judged by criteria remote from his program for development, disillusionment and ineffectiveness occur. Faculty belong to a beleaguered profession. Their salaries have fallen behind even the modest expectations of years past. Their mobility has been curtailed by the increasing scarcity of available positions. They are easy targets these days as more and more colleges cut back faculty for reasons of financial exigency. And all of this is happening to the group that all agree is the heart of the whole enterprise.

How would an ideal program of professional development and assessment be described? The answer is, by placing the faculty member centrally in the planning process. Any number of constituencies must be taken into consideration in the evaluation process (students, department heads, academic deans, peers), but the faculty member must feel that he or she has significant input in determining the criteria for the evaluation and in assuring that the evaluators stick to the "terms" of the development plan. The principal control on the part of the faculty is in the co-authorship of the growth or development plan as such. Department heads and deans will insure that the aims of the college and the disciplines are considered, but the faculty member will determine the particulars of his or her development--of his or her career. And all of this requires many hours of conversation between the faculty member and students, peers, department heads, academic deans, and at the small college, the president. Ultimately, it all gets personal.

Pedagogy, Perquisites and Perceptions

To expect young people to be astute in distinguishing between things as they are and things as they seem to be is unrealistic. Perceptions are always important; they are especially so to young people. The ideal liberal arts college will take care to establish the teaching faculty in environments of perceivable importance. Young people make simple and simplistic equations. How can intellectual enterprises of great pitch and moment be perceived by students as important if they are professed by faculty housed in grubby little offices, marginally considered, and obviously penurious. Why would any student want to accept such a role model? Hopefully, students will learn (as faculty assuredly know) that substance is more important than show. But since perceptions are important, the point here is that the administration at the college striving for excellence will discover real and perceivable ways to establish the faculty in an environment that readily signals to students the importance of teaching and professing and hence of ideas and learning.

Stereotypes

A number of half truths and misconceptions about faculty abound. The troublesome aspects of these chiaroscuro portraits is that there are indeed gray areas. At the ideal college the touchstone of personalization will not allow categorizing any group in the academic family in terms of hasty generalizations or stereotypes. Just as faculty often have handy but unfair apothegms which stereotype administrators, just so administrators have "received truths" and communal aphorisms which stereotype faculty. Objectivity and good will and Arnoldian disinterest will do much to remove unnecessary barriers set up by needless stereotyping.

A common half truth is that college faculty know little about teaching because they know little about learning theory as it applies to young people. It is difficult to respond to such a misconception since one may wonder which learning theory is being referred to. (There have been so many--some relatively harmless, some definitely harmful.) The assertion that "theory" is lacking discounts the lessons of experience. The newly-arrived Ph.D. has been a great many years observing teachers, learning what is good and what is bad about teaching. The idea that college teachers are merely replicas of other college teachers is an unfounded generalization which removes the possibility of any prospective teacher's ever making a judgment about his or her teachers. Too, a very great many have read, usually with considerable caution, the various educational theories as they have come along. Certainly, college teachers must be encouraged always to consider the receivers of the information they convey as well as the information itself. They will translate their scholarship to the classroom. Assuredly there are poor college teachers, and there have been enough who divorce themselves from teaching (focusing almost exclusively on research and publishing) to allow the formulation of the stereotype.

Getting Down to Teaching

Parents, students, and the academy all want the same thing for the student--success. Each of these three interest groups has different definitions for "success," although all definitions converge finally on graduation day. Parents want their children to be happy, to subscribe to the values they associate with a college education (including choice of friends and mates), and to be vocationally successful to get a job. Students want happiness, too, but think more in immediate terms, of the "now." They also want freedom, emotionally and intellectually, just so long as they do not have to abandon their financial and emotional ties to parents. And they, too, want a job or placement in graduate or professional school. The academy through its faculty and administrators wants

49

students to learn the lesson of the academy (in and out of the classroom), including the values which form the basis for the shared vision in the academy, and to mature to a point of emotional and intellectual independence. When these definitions are realized on graduation day, all constituencies feel that they have been "successful." The most important group to realizing this common success is the faculty.

The faculty should know these things about teaching: "success" from the viewpoint of parents, students, teachers and administrators results when teachers

(1) are competent in their callings (the sine qua non of teaching);

(2) exhibit an infectious enthusiasm about their subjects and for their students as they exhibit their expertise in and beyond the classroom;

(3) are willing to make a commitment to each student, to personalize education, to take time to be with students in many contexts; and

(4) are alert to changes in student behavior.

Students often report that their best teachers are those who "are excited about their subjects and interested in me." And, since teachers see students regularly and formally, they must be alert to changes in student behavior. A change in academic performance (low grades) and excessive absences are obvious alterations in behavior. Other changes may be observed, but low grades and excessive absences are easily perceived signals that something is wrong. The formal monitoring of student performance every four weeks (outlined in Chapter Three) is an extraordinary demonstration of the entire academy's being alert to alterations in student behavior. At the ideal college theories of learning and knowledge of student behavior are summed up, then, in a tetralogy of criteria for teaching: the teacher must evidence competence in a discipline, exhibit enthusiasm for the subjects taught, adopt a personal approach to teaching, and monitor closely student behavior. Implicit in the above tetralogy are the ideas that teachers must care for their students, that they do this best when they respond immediately to students' needs, that they must motivate students and not leave them to seek their own level of performance, that they give students freedom to explore without their feeling abandoned, that they praise them, that they keep their roles clearly distinguished, that they have high standards, that they understand that grades are important, and that they take students seriously. For this ideal teaching to take place, students and teachers must come together often in all sorts of ways and in all sorts of places. Administrative policies and faculty programs cannot leave this essential meeting to chance.

Teaching Load

An array of courses splashed across the curricular palette may prove interesting as one observes all of the variations of shade and texture possible, but that array is debatable as a work of art or as ideal undergraduate education practice; in terms of a planned program for personalization, such a palette exhibits little more than colorful chaos. The ordering of the undergraduate's experience into an artistic work of academic success is achieved, to a significant degree, through personalization of the student-mentor relationship, not through proliferation of courses. It is suggested here that a nine-hour teaching load become the standard rather than the twelve-hour load, with the "released time" programmed to bring the faculty members together with students in a meaningful "conversational context"--the conversation focusing on a specific, planned topic or set of topics. The personalization of teaching does not excuse mentors from research or preparation or planning for the time spent with students. Idle chatter or broad philosophical excursions on the nature of things can only serve as a prelude to learning, not learning itself. There must be substance in the conversation. Instituting nine-hour loads would require considerable curricular adjustments at most institutions, and hard assessments as to the purpose of a particular discipline in the undergraduate program and the courses necessary to maintain the integrity of the discipline would have to be made. (Such an exercise is a legitimate and helpful academic exercise in itself.) It is suggested further that a more focused offering for the students will result, a focus often lost through proliferation of courses and the offering of courses which reflect a teacher's interest rather than the interest of a student's mastering the content and vocabulary of a discipline. Proliferation of courses is often the result of subtle promptings to assure faculty security: faculty add courses, oftentimes, to insure their positions. The administration must make it clear that reduction of courses and course loads in order for faculty to spend more time with students will be rewarded and that jobs are secure. The signal must be clear and consistent.

If reducing the courses in the discipline is not a viable way to achieve nine-hour teaching loads, then additions to the faculty will have to be made to achieve the goal of increasing student-teacher contact. Personalization of teaching would thus become an institutional priority: the governing board, the administration and the faculty must want to establish the "conversational context"--the board and administration in terms of allocation of institutional resources (more money for the delivery system) and the faculty in terms of programmed time spent with students. Insuring the conjunction of students and faculty will be universally accepted and practiced as the most approved theory of learning at the ideal college.

Faculty and the Unique Nature of the Academy

The academy some time after World War II, but especially in the Sixties, began to confuse or deprecate a system of values based on common sense and practical tests of worth, opting instead for a system based on speculative theories governed by the dogmas of relativism. The ambient incoherence evident in academic programs across the United States is a result of the extraordinary heterogeneity of vision of the professional inmates behind the murals. More precisely, the incoherence--and hence the loss of distinction and quality--is the result of a polyglot of visions. Diversity and multiplicity of ideas and personalities are much desired in the liberal arts college, but the vision of what the academy is about must be shared by the greater number. If most of the faculty and administrators do not want--in the most fundamental way--the aims of the academy to be realized, those aims will not be--or at least will not be realized satisfactorily. The academy will be, as it is in many places, "all in pieces, [with] all coherence gone." There must be a shared vision of what the academy itself is.

The academy does not like to be "like" anything else. It is unique. Some advance the corporate model as an analogy to the governance of the academy. The analogy will not hold! If it does, it will be an indication that the academy is dead. There are points of correspondence, and one may press the analogy to a certain extent. If, however, the thinking reaches the point where faculty are viewed as employees and administrators as managers, the ideal will have been abandoned in favor of the expedient. If the corporate model were adopted, then students would have to be thought of as products or consumers and "personalization" would become a burdensome cost overrun. If the ideal liberal arts college is to be realized, the ideal must be replicated throughout all levels of the academy, including faculty and administration. Pressed very far, the corporate analogy becomes most embarrassing.

A college is not a participatory democracy, any more than it is a private business. It is something unique. If one must have a model, a hierarchical structure best suits. The educational process itself follows a hierarchical system, from the ladder of learning to the granting of <u>degrees</u>. Hierarchy implies order, levels of responsibility, distinction in rank, and, at its best, reciprocity. If a college becomes so financially strapped that survival is possible only by abandoning the academy in favor of the corporation, it should be allowed to die. If the curators lose their vision of what the academy is and confuse it with a business, the soul of the college will die.

Faculty and the Curriculum

Faculty, ideally, <u>should</u> be extremely sensitive about their prerogatives as guardians of the curriculum. They are the ones primarily responsible for determining, preserving and transmitting that corpus of knowledge, arts and values which make up the treasured heritage which binds all together as a society. They also are responsible for teaching the specific knowledge of the disciplines. In other words, they are responsible for the main business of the liberal arts college. When administrators confuse faculty as personalities with faculty as representatives of the academy, a college is poorly administered. And what confusion would follow if just anyone could determine the curriculum. During the traumatic period of recent memory when faculty at liberal arts colleges were reluctant to abandon their commitment to the liberal arts in face of extreme pressure to do so, one heard all sorts of talk about faculty protecting vested interests, faculty being unable to act because they could not agree or be conclusive, and any number of observations

53

about faculty being too sensitive about their prerogatives as guardians of the curriculum and degree requirements. Faculty at the ideal college, however, will not yield to those who want changes in the curriculum to make the college "streamlined," or "more attuned to the modern world" (a euphemism for smorgasbord offerings), or "vocationally realistic," or "more attractive to the consumer," or even "more like a business." Happily, the liberal arts college is once again "respectable," but the faculty must remain vigilant--holding up the values of the liberal arts curriculum as a constant in a world of shifting ideas and relative values.

Suggestions for a Program for Success

1. Develop a "conversational context" for faculty and students. Among other things, establish a nine-hour teaching load as standard.

2. Provide programs which allow students to participate with faculty firsthand in the process of scholarship and to profit from its rewards.

3. Provide a faculty development program to support faculty members with time and money so they may improve personally and professionally.

4. Develop a method of evaluating faculty that places the faculty member centrally in the planning and evaluating process, a method which relates unambiguously faculty development to faculty assessment.

5. Develop a "conversational context" for faculty and administrators in order to remove harmful stereotypes, avoid disruptive generalizations, and promote a shared vision.

6. Place the faculty in an academy certain of its identity and with faculty controlling the curriculum.

7. Increase significantly the salary for teachers who demonstrate a willingness and talent to "personalize" teaching, who spend meaningful time with students beyond the classroom and office, thus signaling to the faculty what the single most important priority of the teacher should be.

CHAPTER FIVE

ADMINISTRATION

"Pangloss sometimes said to Candide: 'All events
are linked together in the best of all possible
worlds. . .'

'That is well said," replied Candide, 'but
we must cultivate our garden.'"

Voltaire

The most inclusive term in the lexicon of the
liberal arts college is "administration." Nothing
falls outside the purview of "the administration,"
nor should it: fund-raising, admissions, curators,
alumni, and the departments that administer the various
functions of the college, must be considered. Yet
a balancing act of some proportions must be performed
by those who administer. Academics justifiably resent
intrusions into their domains by those not versed in
the vocabularies of their undertakings, but "inclusion"
and "intrusion" are two different terms. Obviously,
administrators must assess, make judgments, and give
directions: they are charged with that responsibility.
They should also inspire. They must achieve their
ends, however, <u>through</u> <u>other</u> <u>poeple</u>, and their skills
as administrators may be measured by their ability
to direct without intimidating, to lead without inter-
fering, to provide ideas without curtailing creativity,
to be decisive without being cavalier. The key to
the success of the administration of the liberal arts
college is the president, the "prism holder" as he
or she is described in Chapter One.

The President

The president at the small, liberal arts college
exerts a disproportionate influence on all that occurs
at the college. It is not simply a matter of hierarchy,
although the Renaissance motto, "as the head is, so
shall the trunk be," applies with all its implications.
It is simply that the obligatory bureaucracy of the
larger university, with all its layered obfuscation
and ponderous process of decision-making, is economically and structurally not possible at the small college.
The above is not a statement of philosophy, but simply
one of fact. And the organizational reality of the
small college, for good or bad, is that the president

is definitively influential in determining the course and character of the college. The college begins to take on the personality of the president, even in the brief space of four or five years. As such, the position is one well suited to the educational entrepreneur, to the highly-motivated person of action who is not afraid to take risks, one who would be uncomfortable enmeshed in the bureaucracy of the larger university. He will be challenged but not intimidated by the knowledge that a particular decision might affect the very existence of the college. With these observations in hand, what should the small liberal arts college look for in a president?

(1) The president will, above all, be concerned with vision, with establishing in his constituency a shared vision of what the mission and goals and promise of the college are. It is worth reiterating that if he cannot create a community of common purpose, he will fail as president. It is for this reason that the metaphor of the inverted prism is so effective in describing his role: he must, as the prism holder, take into consideration all of the personalities, programs and pursuits of the college community and create a community of common vision and purpose. A clear goal of the president is to assemble a number of faculty and staff who, as a cadre of leaders, will champion the mission of the college while supporting the administrative style of the president. It is understood that considerations of style cannot be divorced from considerations of substance, but the point here is that support by a significant number of people of a president's style (his approach to administration) produces harmony. And the cadre must support and promote the mission and goals of the college to relieve the president from tilting at windmills; if the president must always be defining to the constituency the reason for the college's being, he or she will wear out and so will the college.

(2) The president must not only subscribe to the liberal arts college in the fullness of its definition (see Chapter Two), but must also be a partisan, a tireless defender of the faith. He or she will not be swayed by the timid voices advocating easy vocational "fixes," but will have the strength to be pulled by the inevitable chords of practicality without relinquishing the commitment to the liberal arts. The ideal president, in other words, will avoid the either . . . or fallacy. The stipulation that the president

must at rock bottom be a zealous champion of the liberal arts is not mere nostalgia, a yearning for the good old days of Henry Adams. Nor is it simply reactionary. Studies such as the one done by Ellen E. Chaffee of the National Center for Higher Education Management Systems demonstrate that in these days of peril for liberal arts colleges, those colleges which stay true to their liberal arts values and curricula survive while those which do not, fold, or are less successful. In her article entitled "Turn-around Management Strategies: The Adaptive Model and the Constructive Model," Ms. Chaffee says that the "constructive model" of management, i.e., one in which there was a strong adherence to maintaining the mission and goals of the college, was "more resilient" and thus more successful than the "adaptive model" of management, i.e., one in which there were changes in mission and purpose in order to respond to immediate demands of the market-place. Ms. Chaffee does say, however, that the most successful colleges employ both managerial patterns, so long as the "constructive strategy . . . guides the adaptive strategy" (italics ours). In addition, those presidents who keep their eyes on the mission of the college do not view survival as the mission (see page 59 below).

(3) The president must have communicative competence, the full range of "people skills" which allows communication to go beyond the exchange of sounds, gestures and symbols. He or she must communicate substance as well as style: both are important, but the former is essential. The president must be proven by any litmus test of human interaction to be genuine. This president will be incisive but understanding, decisive but empathetic. He or she will be what one commentator calls a "rhetorically sensitive individual." This paragon of presidential virtues will be, after all, human; but it will be the ability to share this humanity--not denying the common frailties that flesh is heir to--that will set apart the ideal president. The chasm between faculty and administration grows wider and wider each year, it seems, and many faculty and many administrators have adopted a stance that the two groups, like Kipling's East and West, can never meet on a common ground but must perforce be adversaries. That is not ideal. The president wanted here will establish trust. From that all else follows.

(4) The president must be willing in policy and practice to make all things personal. "Getting personal"

in this context has no pejorative connotations. This characteristic is simply one aspect of the communicative competence discussed above, but it is such an important aspect that it deserves emphasis. It is a truism of human behavior that when someone feels personally involved, he or she will respond more positively and productively, whatever the context. Personalization as policy, although simple in conception, is difficult in practice. The president must be willing to set aside time to be effective, and since the demands of time on the small-college president are unceasing, he or she must program time to be personal.

(5) The president must believe in teaching, in learning, and in the academy. Too often, faculty, students, staff, libraries, and laboratories are viewed as pawns to be moved, risked, cherished, or discarded in the game of administering. There is nothing wrong with a president's being ambitious, but he or she must not divorce ambition from morals, from academic integrity. After all, a clear system of values and academic integrity forms the foundation for the liberal arts college. The president must share the vision of the love of learning and teaching that motivates the professors of a discipline. And the president must highly regard those doing the professing. There should be evidence of this devotion to the high aims of the academy, that is, devotion to that society of learned persons united in their vision to advance art, science, literature and values in order to improve the lot of humanity.

(6) The president must have extraordinary energy and physical and emotional stamina. As the students say, the president must always be "up". He or she will not be protected by the buffers of bureaucracy. Few waking hours will be free of concerns over enrollment, fund raising, or personnel. The president must constantly cultivate the garden. These constant demands on the emotions and intellect can dim the very vision that made the individual want to be a president in the first place. These demands can deaden a sense of humor, foster skepticism, blunt the personality, and even, alas, compromise the president's integrity. With the energy to carry out the required tasks and with the emotion and intellectual elasticity to remain optimistic about people and learning, the small-college president can make a significant difference in the life of the college. But this opportunity, as ego-satisfying as it no doubt is, can turn to dust if the president becomes emotionally and intellectually tired

and withdraws into a protective shell of administrative regulations and isolation. The creativity and caring will be gone with the lost energy and lost faith.

(7) The president must be a thoughtful risk taker. Administrative styles vary widely. The "caretaker" president must be avoided as surely as the "noble self" president. "Caretaker" here does not mean an "interim" president or "temporary" president. The "caretaker" president is one who weighs all decision and actions on the scales of presumed safety. Nothing risky is ever considered, and being correct or "on the winning side" figures largely in the caretaker's thinking. The caretaker is a rhetorical reflector, reflecting the rhetoric of the moment while waiting to see how the wind will blow tomorrow. On the other hand, the small, liberal arts college can hardly afford the "noble self" president, the megalomaniac who is so confident of his infallibility that he shoots from the hip. This rash actor is usually so certain of his own ideas that no scales are large enough for the ideas and the ego, which are inseparable, to be weighed in. The president who is willing to risk much can do much. The ultimate risk a president at the liberal arts college might have to take is one which would result in the closing of the college. The ideal president at an ideal college with an ideal faculty will not see "survival" as the desired end; he and his governing board and fellow administrators and faculty will assert that unless academic integrity can be maintained, survival is not worth the price of compromising quality. The "great question"--the moment of truth--comes when this question is answered: "If we can't have academic integrity, are we willing to close the college?" The risk taking follows solid counsel and intense consideration. Many points of view are considered. The wider the ramifications of the decision, the more people in the college community will be involved in the discussion. This pattern or style of administration is so fundamentally apropos precisely because it mirrors the environment encouraged at the ideal liberal arts college, that is, one of intellectual and emotional risk taking. Each problem the president encounters will be considered a serious one, virtually a crisis. This approach, certainly, is not "crisis administration," but simply the commitment on the part of the president to be so individual, so personal, as to view each problem as meriting considered attention.

More prosaically and beyond the ideal of risk

taking, the ideal president must be a constant agitator
in all areas of the college, an instigator, an inserter
of ideas, a proactor, not a reactor. Specifically,
he should consistently provide ideas that are supportive
of the mission of the college for all programs, departments and individuals, ideas that will enhance the
quality of those programs, departments and individuals.
And, of course, he must have those skills in dealing
with people that are mentioned above or his ideas
will be rejected or subverted. It is the considered
judgment here that to be effective as an educational
gadfly, as an originator of ideas or--equally important-
-as an inspirer of ideas, the president must program
a conversational context, a way to personalize the
delivery of his ideas, or he will not be successful.
Academics have egos honed to a fine edge and resist
coming into contact with anyone else's whetstone.
But a president who is genuine in his support of the
academy and honest in his dealings with people and,
above all, willing to see his ideas superseded, transmuted, succeed or fail, will be effective with the
greater number of his constituents; and he will be
wise indeed if he insures that credit for successful
implementation of ideas he initiated is shared among
those who respond to the ideas and make them work.
Too, he must not become so enamored of his own ideas
that they begin to take on the quality of infallibility,
issuing forth ex cathedra.

President's Spouse

The spouse of the president should be considered
part of the administrative team, especially at the
small liberal arts college. The "presidential spouse"
is responsible for cultivating the interests of the
college in the multitudinous ways that demand the
talents and interests of the president. The spouse
will be responsible for programs involving faculty,
staff, students, alumni and curators (see below).
Assuredly, the profile advanced here is not one of
a skilled host or hostess, although such skills are
also required. The "presidential spouse" should be
viewed as the co-author of the president's work, evalu-
ated in these terms, and paid a specific salary to
indicate the expectations and the value of the position.
He or she should, without sacrificing individuality,
share the same vision as the president and exhibit
many of the characteristics of the ideal president
outlined above. Moreover, the ideal "presidential
spouse" will complement the president, filling in the

spaces and lightening the load of ever-present responsibilities and concerns which weigh so heavily these
days on any president of a liberal arts college--not
simply or primarily through demonstrations of conjugal
sympathy and support, but through real contributions
based on ability.

The Board of Curators and the President

Every administrative organizational chart indicates
that the college president comes in between the governing board and the rest of the college. At the ideal
college the president will be a link in a communal
chain of common purpose, not something that divides.
The curators (trustees, governors) of a college should
not operate in the vacuum of the board room. A college
president should not insulate the curators from the
life of the college. At every turn the president should
encourage the personal involvement of the curators
in discovering and understanding the programs, policies
and people of the college. Assuredly, this personalization process does not mean that the curators should
assume administrative duties or be involved in the
day-to-day operations of the college. A college administered from the board room is in trouble or on the
way to trouble. But the board members should share
the vision of what the college is and is striving to
be, should share in the mission and goals of the
college, just as do the faculty and administration.
To be able to promote the college in these ways,
curators should be on familiar terms with it.

Each governing board needs a committee on the
care and feeding of the president. This committee
of three or four--it should be small--should be responsible for the primary evaluation of the president,
including developing whatever formats for evaluation
the board might require. This committee should be
prepared to carry on a continual conversation with
the president to determine his or her professional
and personal goals as well as to evaluate performance.
It is uncommonly awkward for the president to approach
the board concerning matters of compensation, and this
committee should relieve the president of this concern.
This committee, after initiating discussions with the
president concerning compensation, should then report
its recommendations to the entire board. The aim of
this committee should be to relieve the president of
any personal financial worries so that he or she can
give individual attention to the concerns of the college.

Allocation of Time. The president should cultivate certain board members beyond the others, not in an attempt to show favoritism or establish a "good ol' boy" network, but to identify those who will have the greatest impact on the college in order to take advantage of their talents, their experience and their philanthropy. He should do the same with faculty and staff. A wise president once asked a novice if the novice could identify the ten persons who would have the most influence in and on the college over the next ten years. The wise president then said, "I bet you spend more time with ten other people who will have little impact on the college than with those you named." The novice had to admit the accuracy of the unexpected response but learned at the same time a valuable lesson in administration. The ideal president will program more time to be with those, including certain curators, who are the obvious leaders and contributors in the college. He will not lose sight of the others, will not slight them, but he will diplomatically and skillfully arrange his time to establish a personal relationship beyond the ordinary with the leaders of the board.

Curator Spouses. The spouses of board members should be included in the "conversational context" in a substantive way during the times set for formal board meetings. For example, the spouses should be present at the annual state of the college address by the president. In addition, during the times the board members are in private sessions, a planned program for the spouses should be in place. It would be especially effective to arrange meetings for the spouses with faculty members, perhaps in areas of interest indicated by the spouses. Visits to the classrooms and laboratories increase the interest and involvement generated by the personal attention paid to spouses. The informal reports given by these spouses to their board member husbands or wives--on the plane or in the automobile, etc., after the meeting--yield demonstrable returns in terms of added commitment to the college and personal curator involvement in its programs. The spouse of the president should play the leading role in this program to involve the spouses of board members in the life of the college.

The Academic Dean

An academic dean is like Sir Thomas Browne's great amphibian half out of the pit. As such, he must be successful in and out of water--even hot water. The ideal dean will apply the common themes of this book to this office: he will (1) insure--above all others---the integrity of the academic program; (2) work closely with the president to create a community with shared vision, focusing primarily on creating a shared vision among the faculty; (3) be an ardent supporter of the liberal arts; (4) program time for personal encounters with faculty and students; (5) avoid the either.... . . or fallacy as he or she negotiates the amphibious role as faculty member and administrator; and (6) translate the system of values which informs the ideal college into everyday policy, a considerable task.

The academic dean should be cautious to maintain the dignity of his office since he is the cornerstone of the entire academic enterprise. This admonition does not suggest that the dean be aloof or remote---far from it. The crux of the matter comes in the relationship between the dean and the president. Too often, at the small, liberal arts college (and even at others), the dean becomes little more than a stepin fetchit for the president. The dignity of the office is lessened as the dean is asked to do chores better suited for an office boy or, at best, an executive secretary. The ideal dean and ideal president will not allow this to happen. The ideal dean will have the rapport with the president that is based on their common understanding and support of the mission of the college and the worth of the academic enterprise they direct. They will both know their respective roles (with the hierarchical implications and differences), but they will be intellectual and professional peers (hopefully friends), each confident enough to risk being told that one or the other is wrong.

The academic dean at the small liberal arts college is the chief "implementer" of administrative policy, most critically in terms of the curriculum and personnel (faculty). He must be skillful in discovering approaches to achieving the programs the president and his staff (including the dean) set as policy. It takes considerable genius to take an idea whose genesis was an administrator and translate that idea into faculty acceptability--and then make it work.

The ideal dean will personalize the academic program by meeting often with students (such as the planned meetings in the academic monitoring program suggested in Chapter Three). Beyond that, he will spend much time with faculty--not in his office--but in their offices and laboratories and classrooms (when invited), creating a conversational context. He will act as an interpreter of the faculty to the administration. He will keep his finger on the pulse of the academic programs, principally as an inspirer and promoter, not as an inspector general. He must, however, as the professoriate itself must, not tolerate incompetence. He must know his faculty so that he can match the available resources with their legitimate professional aspirations. A faculty creating is a happy faculty; the ideal dean will insure a wealth of activity--prompting, encouraging, demanding, leading, promoting--as he creates a community of scholars and artists striving for academic excellence under the aegis of a clear definition of what the college is and where it is going.

Fund Raising

The President's Role. The president described above whose ideas and influence are pervasive throughout the college is as rare as a dry-point etcher or a metaphysician. The rarity becomes more obvious when considering fund raising. The obvious importance of fund raising at the liberal arts college has often resulted in the president's abandoning his role in the academy as he raises money for the academy. Fund raising cannot become the exclusive, or virtually exclusive, enterprise of the president. If he delegates to others the responsibilities for all that goes on in the college, he will have lost his "formulative" influence, his connection to the college. Rather than a thing apart, the ideal president will consider fund raising as part of the dynamics of the college--under the umbrella of personalization. And he must develop with his fundraising staff specific plans to personalize fund raising and to integrate the efforts into the other facets of the life of the college.

Personalizing Fund Raising. An ideal program of fund raising may be achieved by relating fund raising specifically to the mission and goals and programs and people of the college, and by planned personalization of the process. The five imperatives below detail the steps to achieve such a development program.

1. Approach donors on the premise that people, not institutions, give money.

2. Realize that, for the most part, people give

money to particular programs rather than to the institution in general.

3. Consider every gift, regardless of size, as a major gift to the college because the donor will assuredly consider it as such.

4. Educate the donor as to the mission, goals and programs of the college and provide detailed examples (focusing on personal anecdotes) of the success of the college in order to establish rapport and trust in the donor.

5. Develop unique methods of keeping in touch with current givers.

These five guidelines all involve some aspect of personalization. If the individual prospective donor can identify with the mission of the college and feel a part of the program (and trust that the college is in good hands), he or she will be more likely to respond positively. This approach involves face-to-face encounters. Brochures, media campaigns, etc., are peripheral to the meeting of the college representative with the prospective donor. Whoever is the "seller" of the college must be genuine and enthusiastic in supporting the mission of the college and astute enough to match a specific need of the college with a specific interest in the prospective donor. The point is worth repeating: matching a donor's specific interest with a corresponding need is one of the very best ways to personalize fund raising. Establishing this relationship is more important than delivering data about tax benefits or estate management, etc. A program is needed for keeping in touch with current givers to remind them of the specific ways the college is benefiting from their contributions and to reiterate appreciation for the contributions. No one should be left out, from the donors of the least gift to the greatest. The tendency in fund raising to move on to another donor while forgetting the previous one is ill-advised, since the well-informed and suitably-appreciated giver is the best prospect for a future gift.

Models. The four specific models which follow provide suggested approaches to personalizing fund raising:

(1) Model 1: Hall of Sponsors. The prime focus for fund raising should be student scholarships. Not

65

all money is raised for scholarships, of course, but focusing on students as a frame of reference is easily understood by prospective benefactors of the college as evidence that the college's priorities are in the right place. A principal _motive_ for giving to a college is to satisfy an individual or family ego or to perpetuate the memory of someone. Success in fund raising, as noted earlier, involves appropriately matching the prospective donor with a particular need; in this instance, when the "focus" and the "motive" are brought together in a personalized program, success follows. The particulars are these:

A much trafficked hall with ample wall space for display is chosen and designated the "Hall of Sponsors." On the walls will be hung a large picture of a donor of a scholarship with smaller pictures of recipients surrounding it. An amount, such as $25,000, will be established as the minimum amount to sponsor one student and qualify for the Hall of Sponsors. The president and his development staff will then approach the prospective donor with the possibility of establishing a _scholarship that will last forever_, supporting student after student through college, _in the name of the donor or the name of someone he designates_, forever. The donors and their families and friends respond emotionally to the prospect of the donor or his designate being personally identified through the picture in the hall with its well-publicized aim of supporting young people who want a college education. The college will insure that the student recipient is an outstanding student in terms of talent, scholarship, service or leadership.

Beyond this, the college will require the student recipient to contact the donor at least twice a year, by telephone, or in person, to talk about how he or she is doing in college--another example of putting fund raising on a personal basis. The point should be made to these recipients that as alumni they, too, want to establish a scholarship in the Hall of Sponsors. In addition, by showing other students examples of their peers who have been honored as "Hall of Sponsors" scholarship winners, student role models are provided.

(2) _Model 2: The Tie That Binds_. The attempt should be made to bring together for a personal meeting each donor to the college with the individual recipient (or the individual who represents the department, program or activity receiving the gift). The recipient should be prepared to explain the mission and goals

66

of the college and its system of values in general, and explain the impact the gift will have (by way of expressing appreciation) on the life of the individual or the college in particular. The expression of appreciation as a personal expenditure of time and interest from a representive of the college cultivates future giving. A college president may arrange a formal dinner to recognize a representative of a large corporation which has contributed hundreds of thousands of dollars to the college or a student may take a donor of a microscope on tour of the biology laboratory to see the gift in action. In both instances an expenditure of time will be programmed to impress upon the donor the force his or her gift will have in sustaining the mission of the college.

(3) Model 3: Covering the Map. The basis for the model advanced here is matching every donor to the college, regardless of the size of the donation, with a student from the donor's geographical area. The purpose of the match is to have a student meet with the donor to express appreciation for the gift and to let the donor see firsthand a product from the college the donor is supporting. The students who are asked to participate will be articulate in translating the mission and goals of the college into the particular context of the meeting with the donor. Further, the students will be certain to explain how persons or programs (or both) have benefited from the gift. The preparation of these students antecedent to their visits with donors in their "home" areas gives valuable training in a number of skills and develops confidence in these students as they are placed in contexts beyond the academy. The meetings are planned to take place during school holidays, but may take place any time. A variation on this "matching" program is the Newspaper Insert Program, where once again geography and people are pinpointed to aid in fund raising.

(4) Model 4: The Newspaper Insert Program. The small, liberal arts college, especially one geographically isolated, needs broad exposure but is often without the funds to mount a full-scale media blitz to bring the college to the attention of the public. The following suggestion will allow hundreds of thousands of persons to be informed about the college for a relatively small cost. Students and alumni are identified in terms of their geographic origins and matched with a weekly newspaper in the same geographic area. These weekly newspapers are notified that an insert

is to be purchased to run at a particular time. It is generally accepted that the persons who receive weekly newspapers read the inserts while those who receive inserts in the major dailies do not. Once these newspapers are identified, an insert that the college wishes to present to the readers is written and printed following basic format. As the personalizing touch with this insert, however, a particular section within the insert is left for personal statements from students currently in college who live in the area where the newspaper is circulated. Further, the editors of these weekly newspapers are asked to run a feature on the day the inserts are included on a particular alumnus or student in the community who is well known. For the most part, this will be readily agreed to, especially if the college writes the feature and provides the picture. Lastly, and to further personalize the process, an alumnus or giver within the town where the weekly newspaper is located, is approached and asked to pay for the insert. In return for this, that person's name is mentioned in the insert as the person who made the communication possible. The result is an inexpensive way to cover hundreds of towns within a geographic area with general information about the college and personal information about students and alumni from each area.

Students who participate in these fund-raising programs learn in depth the nature and operation of their college and become ardent partisans of the personalities and programs which make up the college. They learn innumerable skills in communication, psychology, salesmanship and interpersonal relations. They profit from the exchange with persons accomplished in a particular field or persons who have a particular interest in the college. Beyond all this, it will be discovered that student participation in these fund-raising endeavors on the substantive level described above aids in retention of students, a most-welcome by-product.

Admissions

The greatest source of funds generated in virtually any college is from student fees and tuition. Admissions and fund-raising thus assume a kinship. An effective recruitment and retention program is an effective fund-raising program. Since so much depends on enrollment figures, the matters of recruitment and retention must be felt as a college-wide responsibility--not the sole responsibility of the admissions office.

The way to achieve this end is to personalize the process, involving students, faculty, staff, alumni and friends in an effort they want to be engaged in. In any event, with a conservative projection of a twenty-five percent decline in high school graduates over the next decade, recruiting will remain a fierce undertaking. The ideal liberal arts college will not lower its standards to seek students unsuited for its particular programs. The "hard sell" approach will be rejected. Students want to attend a college with academic integrity and a clear system of values, confident in its identity. Why, then, does an ideal college often lack an adequate number of students? The problem is in the selling or the recruiting (as any beleaguered recruiter knows all too well); more specifically, the problem is in the process of recruiting. The solution is to apply the prescriptions of personalization to the selling of the college.

Recruiting by Formula. At the outset, the entire college community should be made aware of the factors which influence students to select a college. The most often given reasons--identifiable academic programs, proximity to home, reputation of the college, and consideration of tuition and other costs--are assumed in this model to be secondary and not prime reasons why students decide to attend or not to attend a certain college. The assertion here is that students choose a college principally for emotional (not intellectual) reasons. They respond to the campus setting, to a particular program or activity, to an individual--on an emotional basis; if the response is positive, the college will likely see the student in its classrooms. For the emotional attachment to the college to "take," the whole community has to be ready in individual ways to personalize. Someone at the institution must become personally involved with the student, taking the time to discover the emotional key which will lock the student to the college. A professor of music might tell a potential performer how he or she will fit into the concert band or choir rather than discuss degrees or student aid. A professor of physics might explain to a student interested in astronomy the need for a student assistant at the observatory and detail the responsibilities of such an assistant. It is clear that the entire college community must be marshaled to aid in recruiting. Every student wants to know where he or she fits. Information concerning fraternities and sororities is often more effective in recruiting, alas, than is a clear description of the academic programs. The point is, those who come into contact with the student in the initial stages of recruitment must determine the student's emotional "attraction" or "attractions" to the college and match the attraction with someone at the college who can best display or explain the attraction to the student. From the moment a prospective student is identified, all who are involved in the admissions process must (1) determine the student's interests and predilections, (2) match those interests and predilections to the institutional stimulus (the person or program or activity with which the student will identify), (3) nurture the development of the attraction.

Once the emotional match is made, the formal process of matriculation must not be left to the bureaucratic assembly line. The student should never be inclined to express the common complaint heard throughout academia: "I'm just a number to them." Every student wants to feel important, as if he or she is the only student applying to the college. To personalize the matriculation process even further, the approach here is to develop a "common thread." A prospective student must not be able to say, "If I was so important before I was accepted or before I sent in my room deposit, why wasn't I important afterwards?" At many colleges, the procedure seems to indicate that the college is no longer interested in the student after the college is sure the student is going to attend. If consistent, planned contact is not maintained with the student after the student has made a decision to attend the college, the student will in many instances change colleges. Interest in the student, from first to last, must be consistent and personal. A person at the college, preferably one who knows the vocabulary of the student's emotional interests, is assigned to the student at the outset of the admissions process. This person will be the student's private and personal admissions counselor. The counselor will leave nothing to chance or the bureaucracy but tailor the process to the entering student. This is the second most important part of the entire recruiting process. (The first is identifying and responding to the student's emotional predilections.)

Organizationally, the process of matriculation should be under the management of one coordinator or director. This may result in some unusual administrative flow charts and initial organizational

70

discomfort. It is all too common, however, for matricu-
lating students to discover, not the proverbial ivory
tower but the tower of Babel. From the response to
the first inquiry, to the receipt of the official application, to the acquisition of the transcript and test
scores, to the packaging of the financial aid grant,
to the explanation of courses and programs, to the
housing or assignment of a roommate, the students are
often faced with a number of responses from any number
of offices, all speaking different tongues. Even worse,
there are often significant delays as the different
offices juggle the students' applications. The director
of admissions will assure--preferably through administrative control--that the common thread process is
followed, even through a follow-up process after the
students are admitted. Finally, the formula emerges:
emotional connection plus personalizing matriculation
plus personal admissions counselor equals show in fall:

```
    E.C. + P.M. + P.A.C. = SHOW
    M O    E A    E D O     IN
    O N    R T    R M U    FALL
    T N    S R    S I N
    I E    O I    O S S
    O C    N C    N S E
    N T    A U    A I L
    A I    L L    L O O
    L O    I A      N R
      N    Z T      S
           I I
           N O
           G N
```

Retention. A college should spend as much time
on retaining a student as on recruiting a student.
The Paradigm for Personalization detailed in Chapter
Three is an ideal way to retain students. Beyond this,
toward the close of each academic year, every student
(excluding graduating seniors) should be interviewed
by someone, usually a professional staff member in
admissions, to discuss each student's plans about returning or not returning. Oftentimes, showing this
interest will convince the wavering student who is
considering transferring or withdrawing to return.
Just as often, specific problems surface which the
counselor can address: the ostensible reason a student
gives for deciding to transfer or to withdraw (usually,
"financial problems") is often quite distinct from
the real reason. The trained counselor will know this.
If the "real" reason for dissatisfaction is discovered

and satisfactorily dealt with, the student, more often than not, is retained.

Sometimes it is best for a student to transfer or withdraw. Sometimes a student transfers in spite of the good offices of a counselor. Ideally, once it is discovered that a student will leave, the counselor should be equally energetic in helping the student relocate. Interest in and personal contact with the student should extend throughout the exit interview. This altruism yields pragmatic returns. The departing students oftentimes discover that the grass is not greener in another grove of academe and return to the place which showed such personal interest in them. Too, even if the students do not return, they may very well recommend the college to a prospective student. Finally, it is good to remember that every student retained is a successful venture in fund raising.

Alumni

Alumni who are convinced that the institution from which they got their degrees and with which they are identified professionally and socially is progressively getting better will be more enthusiastic supporters of the college. Providing alumni newsletters, contexts for nostalgic gatherings, and other services is important and part of the common texture of alumni policy. Effectively demonstrating to alumni that their alma mater has quality programs and is always striving for excellence is the best policy, however. The way to get the message across is through personal contacts. The logistics of delivering this message to the alumni personally is time-consuming, but the returns for personalizing the process are many. For example, it will soon be discovered that alumni have resources to offer beyond financial resources. The expertise in the myriad fields and enterprises of alumni is a significant resource. If they can be convinced to share their expertise by participating in some significant program of the college, the college will profit in two ways: (1) it will benefit immediately from the fruits of the graduates' expertise, and (2) it will benefit from the graduates' strengthened commitment to the college as they become personally and therefore emotionally involved.

The ideal college will emphasize above other alumni programs the involvement with students in curricular or co-curricular programs. The involvement will not be left to chance. If alumni can be brought together with undergraduates in a context where the students can benefit from the meeting, the alumni will develop an emotional attachment to the college far beyond the usual associations with the alma mater. The students will benefit from the expertise and the association beyond the walls.

The Preceptor Program. The planned bringing together of alumni with students might be called the Preceptor Program. Alumni in specific fields of expertise would be matched with students aspiring to enter these fields. A pre-law student could be matched with a lawyer, a business administration student with a businessman or corporate executive, an art student with an artist or director of a museum, a pre-medical student with a physician--and the list could go on. The students in such a program see firsthand the life work they are currently committed to, will be inspired to even greater commitment or to change their vocational goals. Either way, much has been learned. The preceptor, the alumna or alumnus, through this personal response to the college, will become fundamentally involved with the college and its programs. The preceptor's level of financial support will increase in proportion to the involvement with the student and the student's program of study.

Alumni and Governance. Alumni should be included on the governing board of the ideal liberal arts college. The formal structure of the Alumni Association will be strengthened as representative alumni learn firsthand about the operation of the college. A level of understanding and a perception of the realities of the workings of the college are conveyed to the alumni at large by the alumni representatives to the board. Oftentimes, alumni expectations exceed the resources to realize the expectations. Alumni on the board are not only responsible for generating ideas, but also for seeing them implemented. An advisory board of alumni, drawn from the Alumni Association, is too remote from the governance of the college. The distance is often matched by the distance of alumni interest. Alumni can have significant input if they are represented on the governing board (curators, trustees). Alumni will make significant contributions in many ways if given the chance to participate on this level.

Suggestions for a Program for Success

1. Admit the disproportionate influence exerted by the president of the liberal arts college and insure that he is

    a. a person of vision who can create a community of shared vision;

    b. a partisan of the liberal arts not easily swayed by vocational "fixes";

    c. an advocate and practitioner of the personal approach, with the communicative skills ("people skills") to be effective;

    d. a person who believes in the academy and esteems learning and the professors of learning;

    e. a thoughtful risk taker, an academic entrepreneur who avoids the either . . . or fallacy and values academic integrity above survival; and

    f. a person endowed with great energy and emotional stamina.

2. Insure significant involvement by the governing board but avoid the intrusion of board members in the administering of the college.

3. Secure an academic dean who is at once an adept implementer of administrative policy and a dedicated interpreter of faculty concerns.

4. Develop a planned program of personalization for fund raising (such as the five-point approach on p. 64 , with specific models on pp. 65-68).

5. Involve the entire college community in recruiting by personalizing the approach based on the premise that emotions not intellect lead students to choose a college.

6. Develop a thorough program to retain students, such as the Paradign for Personalization (see Chapter Three), paying particular attention to exit interviews.

7. Involve alumni significantly in the programs of the college (such as the Preceptor Program) and include them on the board of governors.

CHAPTER SIX

THE CHURCH

> "'What is truth?' said jesting Pilate; and would not stay for an answer."

Francis Bacon

There is considerable naïveté in Richard John Neuhaus's statement that because "God's revelation in Christ . . . is uniquely realistic because it is uniquely real, that is to say, uniquely true," that Christianity (with its Judaic antecedents) should be politically introduced into the public square. Neuhaus's yearning for an America governed by this "truth"--however he may abhor the inquisitorial chambers of Spain or the banalities of Jerry Falwell--is but a genteel version of making the Bible the law of the land. But Neuhaus in his book The Naked Public Square demonstrates that a valueless context for the business of society is unrealistic: a secular divorcement of religious beliefs and attitudes from the public square is neither possible nor desirable. The private, church-related, liberal arts college is the ideal and appropriate staging area for placing persons committed to a particular set of values based on religious principles into the public arena. The model presented here is formed from the broad traditions of Christian religion, but the generalizations could be translated into any religious context. The point is that the church-related college does provide an obvious setting for a value-based education. The Christian, church-related, liberal arts college will quietly but confidently promote the Pauline virtues of faith, hope and charity, translating all three virtues--but essentially "love"--into "caring" for the student. The manifestation of a Christian atmosphere will best be seen in the creation of an environment where concern for others takes precedence over the demands of self. The Golden Rule in action will be preferred over pronouncements of piety and the promulgation of rules and strictures. The pre-eminent role model will be Jesus Christ. The way institutionally to establish this desired atmosphere of caring is through the planned program of personalization much discussed in previous chapters.

The church-related liberal arts college distinguishes itself (and justifies itself) by offering a system of values within which students can explore,

rebel against, reject, synthesize, or accept whatever
values they ultimately profess. The ideal academy
per se encourages intellectual and emotional exploring,
doubting and risk taking, but the Christian academy
provides a constant buffer of security for the questing
and questioning students. The Christian context
(Jewish, Hindu, Muslim, etc.) insures that while students in their various disciplines are pursuing the
"how" of things, the "why" of things will not be overlooked. The fear that a religious value system will
stifle intellectual curiosity and freedom is not, his-
torically, without foundation; the maintenance of the
strictest levels of academic freedom, of freedom of
inquiry and expression, and a Christian-based system
of values need not be mutually exclusive, however.
In fact, there is far greater academic freedom in exploring an idea from both a secular and non-secular
point of view--if the thinking is not prescribed or
proscribed. If inhibitive orthodoxies intrude upon
the free investigation and exchange of ideas, the
church-related college is not ideal--not the model
proposed here. Finally, the Christian, liberal arts
college will exude an atmosphere of optimism based
on the assurances of a risen Lord, a quality of joy
which permeates the learning and living on campus.

Improving Relations with the Church

There is no mysterious formula guaranteeing im-
proved relations between the church and the church-
related college. Like true and lasting friendships,
what works well for one may not work for another.
The hierarchy and individuals in a church base their
judgments about their church-related institution on
the individual experiences with the institution. Without question, the most important single factor in improving relations with the church is a commitment by
the college to perpetuate such a relationship. The
college must want to be church-related. For that reason, it should be policy to establish a "conversational
context" between the church and the college.

The commitment of the college to the church must
be based on improving the quality of the learning experiences of the students rather than upon securing
increased financial support from the church. When
the former is the desired goal, the latter will follow.
Until a college believes that its programs must provide
"value-based" learning, it will remain in a condition
in which it must constantly explain and defend its

affiliation with the church. The president of the college, most of all, must be truly convinced that a strong relationship with the church enhances the college's educational opportunities. The following suggestions outline a program to establish a lasting and mutually beneficial relationship between the church and its college:

(1) A context should be established where students and faculty engage in substantial conversations on a continuing basis in the pursuit of ideas, knowledge, and values. There is a direct relationship between quality and the amount of time that faculty spend interacting with students beyond the classroom. Faculty members who are enthusiastic about their work and who, informally as well as formally, transmit attitudes and values serve as role models.

(2) Christian values should be emphasized in all collegiate activities and publications. The mission statement should be specific with respect to the college's commitment to Christian values.

(3) An administrator who works closely with the president should be appointed as a director of church relations. He would serve as the principal resource person on campus for all churches to contact when they want information about the college. It would be advantageous if this administrator were an ordained minister.

(4) The president of the college should be visible in the churches which support the college, especially during the first years of his tenure.

(5) Special programs for churches should be provided. Administrators, faculty and students could speak to congregations, Sunday school classes, youth groups, etc. The college bands, choirs, performing groups, etc., could schedule tours to the churches.

(6) Children of ministers in the church should be given a special tuition rate.

(7) If at all possible, an amount equal to the monies received from the churches through apportionment of their annual revenues should be spent on scholarships, especially insuring scholarships for students from these churches.

(8) The campus should be promoted as the meeting

79

place of the churches when they hold their convocations or conferences. The delegates or representatives of the churches gain a familiarity with the campus and its programs that yields many positive benefits upon their return to their home churches.

(9) Ordained ministers of the church should be members of the governing board of the college.

(10) The college should keep the churches regularly informed about the college. Articles for church newspapers, bulletins, newsletters, etc., should be provided by the college. Mailings about special events should be sent to pastors and church congregations.

The above examples are a few ways to strengthen the relationship between the church-related college and its sponsoring church. The church is considered the principal constituency and a starting point for recruiting. The relationship should be a matter of pride; and although there is a strong affiliation, it should be clear that the church does not control the college. The college must remain independent to pretend to academic freedom. Once these matters are made clear, the faculty will no longer be skeptical about close ties with the church and the students will not fear being proselytized. A program with a clear commitment to academic integrity and an equally clear commitment to a system of values will then be in place for the church to support.

Suggestions for a Program for Success

(1) Establish a clear system of values based on an understanding and promotion of the beliefs and traditions of the sponsoring church.

(2) Translate the Christian virtues of faith, hope and love (or similar virtues in other pantheons) into a planned program for personalization, equating these virtues with "caring".

(3) Maintain academic freedom and an atmosphere which promotes the free and bold exchange of ideas, popular and unpopular, while unabashedly identifying with the sponsoring church.

(4) Insure that church sponsorship does not mean church control.

(5) Develop a "conversational context" between individuals in the college and individuals in the church to demonstrate the mutual benefits of the church-college relationship.

CHAPTER SEVEN

INSTITUTIONAL INTENTIONS

"I see it feelingly."

Gloucester in <u>King Lear</u>

"Common sense is tacit reason," said William
Hazlitt, and the approach in this little book has been
to outline a program for success for the liberal arts
college based on common experience "called up for the
occasion." In its insistence on a personal approach
in all areas of endeavor it has placed the emotions
or feelings centrally in the formula for success.
It has posited an environment where the proper concern
is with the ideal translated into a quest for quality
and where values are certain and unambiguous. The
ideal college thus envisioned has a clear identity,
a personality, animated by the partisanship of its
community sharing a vision of its mission and goals.
It includes <u>time</u> as an allocated resource and insists
that time spent with students is time best spent.
It marks each student as its own, agreeing with Newman
that a college is "an Alma Mater, knowing her children
one by one, not a foundry, or a mint, or a treadmill."

The Dust Cloud Hypothesis or Nothing Succeeds Like Success

In one account of the origin of the universe,
the planets and stars were formed from immense collec-
tions of dust particles floating in space. This star
dust was, and is, made up of all sorts of elements:
Hydrogen, helium, oxygen, carbon, etc. These elements,
it is said, slowly coalesced into chemical combinations,
ultimately forming--in about a billion years--into
stars and their satellites. A central question in
this hypothesis is, "What is it that collects these
dust particles into clouds, thus starting the process
of coalescing and forming stars and planets? Professor
Lyman Spitzer believed it was the "pressure of light."
The origins of the ideal college are analogous, with
the dust particles of countless concerns coalescing
into a solar system of learning. The "pressure of
light," i.e., the desire to know, the beckoning of
intellectual and spiritual frontiers, has formed into
three satellites, namely, the parents, the students,
and the college--all circling the sun of success.
"Success" in all its definitions is the life-giver

to the entities orbiting it.

The analogy is too elaborate, but ah, what possibilities. The faculty and administration at the ideal college will understand that there are three groups of stellar importance in determining programs and policies for students: parents of students, the students themselves and the college awaiting students. All of these groups, if closely questioned, want the same thing for those attending the college--success. To be sure, each defines success differently, but they all circle the sun. And when the needs of the groups are clearly defined by programs and policies so that each feels satisfied, then there is harmony of spheres. But how does each group define "success"? Each satellite would say that "success" involves any number of things, but one may simplify to a triumvirate of considerations.

Parents want their children (1) to be happy, (2) to acquire acceptable friends and mates, and (3) to get a good job upon graduation. These seem to be stark items for defining success, but there are many assumptions to be considered. Parents expect happiness to derive from the immediate benefits of college life, social and academic, and expect evidence that their offspring are taking advantage of "the best years of their lives." They assume that the curriculum and the academic program and the broader benefits derived from a system of values and contact with mentors of stature will contribute to future happiness, too. Parents also want their children to establish friendships, many of which undoubtedly last for a lifetime, with young people of similar training, values and lifestyle. They also want their children to find mates with similar characteristics. These parents are not snobs or elitists; they are just parents. Finally, they want their children to be independent and secure upon graduation. They want their children to have jobs or to be admitted to graduate or professional school (preludes to even more prestigious jobs). They assume that at the liberal arts college their children will be taught those things which "foster the shared vision and knowledge that binds us together as a society," but they talk about jobs.

Students paint a similar triptych, but with obvious differences. On each side of the central panel is (1) a desire for happiness and (3) the expectation of a job upon graduation. In the middle is (2) the

desire to be free without risk. Students find happiness
in the freedom from their parents while benefiting
from their financial support. They also want to have
fun, to enjoy the "now"; but when asked why they are
in college, most say they are preparing for a job
(or graduate or professional school). They need room
to explore without losing sight of boundaries: the
curriculum should give them room to experiment while
holding up specific expectations; the college community
should give them contexts to explore socially and
spiritually, too, but with a clear system of values
in place and role models of stature at hand to form
a safety net. The students and parents both place
"success" in relatively short-term categories. The
college defines "success" in short-term and long-term
ways, but the focus is on long-term expectations.
The college expects its students (1) to become familiar
with a particular system of values, (2) to develop
the skills of a discipline or vacation, and (3) to
learn those things which bind all together as a society,
i.e., to profit from the liberal arts curriculum.

Institutional Intentions

The ideal and the pragmatic come together when
the vision of the ideal is put into practice, i.e.,
when the idea of an ideal liberal arts college is made
policy and practice, when vision is converted into
action. In order for the vision to be fully realized,
it must be translated into modes of action; the intentions of the visionaries (those sharing the vision)
need to be made clear. "Institutional intentions"
are the practical manifestation of the ideal that has
already been subscribed to by the greater number of
the college community. As these intentions are institu-
tionalized by becoming policies and programs, however,
they are now promoted as items for common experience:
everyone in the college community should know and be
a part of them. These "institutional intentions" must
be reduced to understandable language, clearly explained, and regularly discussed by all associated with
the college. In other words, as the vision becomes
policy, it must be accurately represented in language
accessible to all.

Final Suggestion for a Program for Success

Take great care to formulate the vision of what the college is and aspires to be into programs for action (institutional intentions), in language accessible to all.